Harmonies & *Hurricanes*

Color and Line
in Japanese Quilts

Kumiko Sudo

THE QUILT DIGEST PRESS
NTC/Contemporary Publishing Group

The equinoctial gales were this year particularly violent. Then came a day when the whole sky grew black, and an appalling typhoon began. It would have been bad enough wherever one had been to see every tree stripped of its leaves just when they were at their loveliest, every flower stricken to the earth; but to witness such havoc in an exquisite garden, dew-pearls unthreaded in an instant and scattered upon the ground, was a sight calculated to drive the onlooker well nigh into madness. As time went on, the hurricane became more and more alarming, till all was lost to view in a blinding swirl of fog and dust. But while she sat behind tightly closed shutters in a room that rocked with every fresh blast, it was with thoughts of autumn splendours irrevocably lost rather than with terror of the storm that the Empress's heart was shaken. . . . Even indoors the wind was so violent that screens would not stand up. Those which usually surrounded the high dais were folded and stacked against the wall. There, in full view of anyone who came along the corridor, reclined a lady whose notable dignity of mien and bearing would alone have sufficed to betray her identity. This could be none other than Murasaki. Her beauty flashed on him as at dawn the blossom of the red flowering cherry flames out of the mist upon the traveller's still sleepy eye. It was wafted towards him, suddenly imbued him, as though a strong perfume had been dashed against his face. She was more beautiful than any woman he had ever seen.

From *The Tale of Genji*, Chapter X,
by Murasaki Shikibu, translated by Arthur Waley

Library of Congress Cataloging-in-Publication Data

Sudo, Kumiko.
    Harmonies and Hurricanes: color and line in Japanese quilts / Kumiko Sudo.
    p.   cm.
    Includes bibliographical references.
     ISBN 0-8442-2661-0
     1. Quilting.   2. Quilting—Patterns.   3. Appliqué.   4. Appliqué—Patterns.
     5. Miniature quilts—Japan.   6. Color in textile crafts.
     I. Title.
    MTT835.S793   1998
    746.46'0952—dc21

                                                 97-43753
                                                CIP

Editorial and production direction by Anne Knudsen
Book design by Kim Bartko
Cover design by Monica Baziuk
Project editing by Gerilee Hundt
Technical editing and drawings by Kandy Petersen
Quilt photography by Bill Bachhuber
Fabric photography by Sharon Hoogstraten
Manufacturing direction by Pat Martin

Published by The Quilt Digest Press
A division of NTC/Contemporary Publishing Group, Inc.
4255 West Touhy Avenue, Lincolnwood (Chicago), Illinois 60646-1975, U.S.A.
Printed in Singapore
International Standard Book Number: 0-8442-2661-0
18 17 16 15 14 13 12 11 10 9 8 7 6 5 4 3 2 1

Contents

Harmonies & Hurricanes

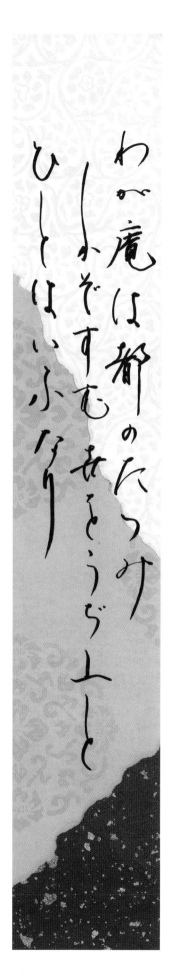

At my cottage on Mount Uji, I enjoy a quiet life in the beauty of nature. I see deer drinking water at a brook and hear birds sing in the woods. I have nothing to worry about. How calm my soul is! Yet they say I am escaping from the world with apprehension, sorrow, and prejudice.

A *waka* poem by Kumiko Sudo. Inspired by *Hamlet Among the Hills*, page 79.

Acknowledgments

I first began collecting antique Japanese *kimonos* and *obi*—the decorative sash that women use to hold the *kimonos* together—about twenty-five years ago, when I still lived in Japan. It was not until I came to America that I thought of using them in my work. I decided to create a series of quilts that would use Japanese culture as its foundation so that I might be able to share some of the history and the beauty of Japan with my fellow Americans.

The numerous pieces of silk I used to make the quilts in *Harmonies & Hurricanes* came from *kimonos* and *obi* that once belonged to members of my family and to friends. I wish to acknowledge all of these dear people and give them my thanks, for without their generosity in sharing with me some of their personal treasures, this book would not have been possible.

Kumiko Sudo

Land of Harmonies & Hurricanes

Japan, in its traditions, arts, and aesthetics, is a land of contrasts and ambiguities. An island country, Japan enjoys four distinct seasons, and the climate, for the most part, is quite temperate. When we think of Japan, an image that comes to mind is of delicate cherry blossoms, the national flower, gently swaying in the spring breeze. Yet as much as the cherry blossom is a sign of spring, devastating, cyclonic storms or hurricanes are all too frequent in late summer and early fall. Throughout Japan's history, these typhoons have influenced its development, its lifestyle, and its culture. They have given the Japanese a stoic reverence of nature's awesome powers as well as a deep appreciation of the beauty and fragility of life. The alarming contrast between the mildness of spring and the cruelty of fall provides insight into the nature of the Japanese people through the ages. They are able to accept both extremes and live with them in perfect harmony, starting afresh when disaster strikes. As we will see, this reverence of polarities—peace and chaos, stillness and passion, harmonies and hurricanes, exists in Japanese art. It is dramatically present in the quilts of Kumiko Sudo.

Several of the quilts in *Harmonies & Hurricanes* are inspired by the courtly tradition of the Heian period, as depicted in *The Tale of Genji*. This epic novel was written more than a thousand years ago by Murasaki Shikibu, a noblewoman of Kyoto. As well as being a poetic chronicle of the loves, intrigues, successes, and failures of court nobles, *The Tale of Genji* is a celebration of beauty, as viewed in nature and as portrayed in courtly life. The stories that accompany such quilts as *Lady Kaguya* (page 33), *Picture Scrolls* (page 37), *Poetry Party at Court* (page 63), and *Ladies in a Fine Snow* (page 91) conjure wonderful pictures of a period during which appreciation of nature's beauty was a mark of refinement. Those images are brought to life by the quilts that add color, dimension, and spirit to that lost, gentle world.

The Japanese word for harmony—*wa*—has its origins in one of the primary principles of Shintoism, the ancient Japanese religion. It teaches that peaceful, harmonious relations must exist among human beings and between human beings and nature in order for everything and everybody to stay in balance, prosper, and fulfill their purpose. The ultimate goal of *wa* permeates and colors every facet of Japanese culture and art.

Picture the serenity of the Japanese tea ceremony, a tradition that reaches back to the fifteenth century. Gracefully dressed in beautiful *kimonos*, guests delicately taste the tea and admire the tea cups and utensils. Yet behind this seemingly effortless social engagement is an age-old ritual for which participants receive years of formal training. Demanding the highest levels of mental control and discipline, the purpose of the tea ceremony is to sharpen the aesthetic sense, calm the spirit, and reach a deep harmony with the universe. For the Japanese, flower arranging, too, is an exercise in aesthetics that requires

Fly, Cranes, Fly!

formal training. Through the rituals of *ikebana*, the Japanese seek to achieve harmony with nature, and, by abiding by the strict disciplines of the art, develop good character and morality. In arts as wide ranging as calligraphy, *Noh* theater, garden design, and the martial arts, such as *karate, judo,* and *kendo,* the same sense of beauty and perfection as a means of achieving tranquillity and happiness is apparent. All involve formal, prescribed rituals that demand a concentration of mental and physical energy, and all seek an effect of peace, simplicity, and harmony.

Sacred Horse

As you examine the quilts in *Harmonies & Hurricanes*, notice how, despite the use of vibrant, swirling colors, harmony is always achieved. In *Fly, Cranes, Fly!* (page 53), the crane is a motif for peace, atonement, and longevity. With dramatic patterns and vivid colors, the overall effect is vigorous and dynamic, yet supremely harmonious. *Sacred Horse* (page 43), evokes the brilliance and energy of the *samurai.* The horse charges forward, full of

From Master to Pupil: Japanese Traditions in Learning Hand Crafts

The ways in which the Japanese learn the techniques and styles of a hand craft have not changed in more than a thousand years. The tradition is based on a feudal relationship—that of master and pupil. In arts as diverse as the tea ceremony, flower arranging, Japanese painting, pottery, gardening, and carpentry, precise techniques, philosophies, and traditions are handed down from master to pupil and are firmly and loyally kept.

In the tea ceremony, for example, it is traditional for the master and pupils to make a study of their guests several weeks in advance. They prepare flowers, tea service, and confectionery according to the tastes of their guests. Through very particular rituals, they purify the tea room, the garden, and the tea water as they await their guests. Master carpenters originally belonged to the royal family, to *shogun* families, or to major temples. In the building of temples and shrines, they used such precise techniques that the structures they created held together without nails and had not even the slightest flaws. The techniques that helped them attain such perfection have passed safely from generation to generation because of the master-pupil relationship.

Though quilting did not become popular in Japan until the 1970s, it is no exception to the Japanese tradition of learning hand crafts. There are patchwork schools all around the nation, and most achieve their success through the master-pupil relationship. The master teacher will have a certain style and very particular techniques that the pupils will learn to imitate. Taught to the highest possible standards of perfection, skills are handed down, just as in other Japanese hand crafts. However, as in all arts through the ages, there are "lone wolves" in the Japanese quilting world who have their own unique ideas and artistic sensibilities. Kumiko Sudo's work proves that she is one of the most brilliant exceptions to the rule.

life and spirit, reminding us that life is short. Yet this bold image is held in check by the circular crest on the right—the carriage wheel depicted here implies continuity, a symbol of eternity. In *Temari* (page 59), inspired by a children's song, the rush of color, movement, and fluidity all create a sense of the joy of childhood and a oneness with nature, as the balls fly gaily into the air.

Temari

Color and Line in
Harmonies & Hurricanes

Kumiko Sudo is admired the world over for her flawless sense of color and line. Here are some of her observations on the inspiration behind her color choices and quilt layouts in *Harmonies & Hurricanes*.

Raging Sea

Raging Sea, *page 29*

Here, two ships sail through a stormy sea, symbolizing Japan breaking out of its feudal past and, after centuries of isolation, reaching out into the world. Waves surge from below and lightning strikes from above as the raging winds in the top right corner toss the two ships around in the tumultuous sea. The thunderous clouds are broken by blue rays of hope, a color with universal appeal. I tried to display the movement of the waves by using solid colors and curved lines. In contrast, the triangles represent new lands, safe and steady, though unknown. The log cabin pattern in the bottom right corner symbolizes America, land of promise.

Raging Sea has special meaning for me. It is the first quilt I made after arriving in the United States and symbolizes my own inward struggles and my hopes as I embarked on a new life.

Awakening, page 31

In *Awakening* I wanted to convey an epic theme— the dawn of civilization in Japan, the land of the rising sun. The dominant color in the quilt is red, a color that always arouses visual sensation. I have used about twenty different shades, as red slowly changes into orange. Light shines from left to right at the top of the quilt, like Aurora's fan in the sky. In contrast, the dark grays at the bottom of the quilt represent a cave, symbolizing the new nation that the light of civilization is just beginning to penetrate. Spiral steps of blue fabrics separate Aurora's fan from the cave, expressing the notion of light going deeply into the dark land of early Japan.

Awakening

Lady Kaguya

Lady Kaguya, *page 33*

A figure of Japanese legend, Lady Kaguya ascends to heaven, leaving the earthly world behind her. Sadly, she sails through the sky, her layered *kimono* of many colors around her and the light of heaven shining upon her. Below, pale and fading into the distance, is the garden Lady Kaguya has left behind. To the left, the red of her *kimono*—a color associated with nobility—fades in and out of the clouds to symbolize the loss of her worldly status. On the outer layer of her *kimono*, the undying bird, the phoenix, represents her eternal life and happiness in heaven. I turned up a small portion of the bottom of her *kimono* to emphasize the graceful figure flowing away like the wind. The clouds and the moon reflect some of the colors of her *kimono*, symbolizing Lady Kaguya's acceptance into heaven.

Ladies in Waiting

Ladies in Waiting, *page 35*

Inspired by the courtly traditions described in *The Tale of Genji, Ladies in*

Waiting depicts the gorgeous decorative *kimonos* of court noblewomen. In a blaze of color, the long flowing *kimonos,* all in multiple shades and layers, rustle against each other as the women move between partitioned rooms. In this quilt, I enjoyed playing with geometrical shapes—triangles, rectangles, squares, and pleats—that come together to create an illusion of movement.

Fly, Cranes, Fly! page 53

Fly, Cranes, Fly!

For this quilt, also titled *New Freedom,* I used a very different color palette than for any other in *Harmonies & Hurricanes.* Here, the dominant colors are black and white, at opposite ends of the color spectrum. For the crane at the bottom of the quilt, I used a combination of different degrees of white, separated by thin lines of stronger color. For the second crane I chose shades of black, a traditional Japanese color. To soften the black, the blue fabric around the wing provides a feeling of roundness. The softly colored hexagons in the background are the gardens, mountains, and lakes far below the free-flying cranes. On both birds, the upper portions of the wings use sharp angles to harmonize with the sharpness of the birds' beaks. The crane is the Japanese bird of freedom, and by creating images of birds in flight, I wished to express my hope that all people are free to make the world a warmer place.

Kumiko Sudo in her studio

An Interview with Kumiko Sudo

Penny McMorris: You have written that you begin your designs by sketching, then choose color. Can you describe your design process?

Kumiko Sudo: When I encounter a particular fabric or any beautiful item that makes a great impression on me, I may make a rough sketch of a design. Then I work on refining the design, scribbling on sheets of paper. Finally, I develop a full-size design on a large piece of paper. This design serves as a "pattern" for me.

Penny McMorris: Your quilts usually tell a story.

Kumiko Sudo: When I design a quilt, I compose a story along with it. For example, in *Raging Sea* (page 29), the first quilt I made after moving to the United States, I created a turbulent seascape showing boats and waves pulled in two directions. This symbolized the inner struggle I was going through—I longed for my past life in Japan and yet was excited about beginning a new life in the United States.

Penny McMorris: Your emigration from Japan to the United States in 1985 was such a long move, away from family and friends. In a way it was not unlike American pioneer women moving across the United States during the mid-1800s to settle new territories. These women often made quilts with scraps of clothing of loved ones. You also made quilts using kimono *silks worn by members of your own family. Can you tell me how using these silks made you feel?*

Kumiko Sudo: It may seem that I was making quilts from those *kimono* fabrics to capture memories of my family. And some of these old *kimono* pieces do bring me some fond memories of my childhood. I remember my aunt, for example, and the scent of her powder when she took her *kimono* out of her dresser—memories like these race through my mind like pictures in a revolving lantern.

But the memories a particular fabric may bring are only momentary. And they usually do not have anything to do with why I choose a particular fabric to use in a design. I choose fabrics for the way they will help me tell a story or set a mood, rather than for any personal memory the fabrics may suggest.

Penny McMorris: I know you have collected thousands of pieces of fabric that you can choose from as you design. How do you begin composing a color scheme for a quilt?

Kumiko Sudo: Choosing color is extremely important as I develop a design. My color scheme appears in my mind very naturally from the beginning as I develop the title and story for the design.

Sometimes the season affects my color choice. When I feel a gentle spring wind, for example, it may suggest pastel colors. At other times my mood determines the colors I want to use. If I'm in a calm and tranquil mood, I may want to use dramatic color combinations.

We are surrounded by colors. But beautiful color schemes do not suggest themselves immediately. With some training, and a sensitivity to your surroundings, you can begin to feel color all around you—in voices and words, in people's attitudes, even in the food you eat. Meeting pleasant people might suggest pink, blue, or cream. After a concert, you might feel lime green, or even a dramatic red. When you feel the cold, wintry wind, it may make you think of gray and black, or it could suggest the red of a fireplace.

Penny McMorris: Colors seem to tell you a story. Do you use particular colors for the symbolic meaning they have for you?

Kumiko Sudo: I love red. I associate red with the sun, fire, blood—all important factors in life. Because I associate red with life, different colors of red represent different strong emotions to me: happiness, tears, celebrations, for example. In Japanese history, red has always been a precious color, loved by nobility, because to turn white silk to red it took so many safflowers to make the dye. Safflowers were rare plants that had to be imported all the way from Egypt and Turkey.

Black is the color made up of all other colors—it represents the unity of colors. Black used in clothing traditionally could indicate nobility. It also represents the end of life. Another color that was traditionally used to represent nobility is purple. In Japan, during the Heian period, the nobility loved the color purple. They dyed *kimono* fabrics with the plant called *murasaki*, which means purple. Purple wisteria blossoms, with great fragrance, represent the sense of beauty of those ancient times. I use purple for figures of nobility or scenes of dusk and sunset.

Green represents growth and long life. Green bamboo and pine are often used as symbols in Japan. Bamboo symbolizes fast growth. The way it is cut horizontally symbolizes unity. Pines stand for long life because pine trees live for hundreds of years. Both green plants are familiar motifs used in *kimono* design.

Penny McMorris: Many quilt makers find working with color one of the most challenging aspects of the design process.

What advice do you give to your students who struggle to develop color schemes?

Kumiko Sudo: First of all, know your own heart and mind. Arrange the colors that you would most like to work with on a table. Then arrange them on your design. Take as much time as you need, until you are satisfied with the result. If you can't decide, relax and do something else for a while to clear your mind. Then come back and look at it again.

Penny McMorris: Do you follow your own advice? What do you do to "clear your mind" when working on your own designs? Do you meditate?

Kumiko Sudo: To clear my mind, I enjoy being outside, working in the yard and garden. I observe the mist on the hills, look at the beautiful changes in the sunset sky, watch the leaves running in the wind, listen to my favorite music under a big tree, talk with my friends or even write nursery tales or play with animals. All of these things are part of my meditation.

Penny McMorris: You have written that you choose "major colors" to best suit the spirit of the work. In your quilt Autumn Poetry *(page 87), can you describe the steps you took in developing the color scheme?*

Kumiko Sudo: In *Autumn Poetry* I wanted to make a magnificent floral arrangement on the vast sky. It was not to be a pretty little bouquet of daffodils or chrysanthemums, but instead a huge and beautiful branch from a big plum tree extending out into the universe. The flowers in *Autumn Poetry* are the princesses in red, with blue added for balance.

Penny McMorris: The four basic elements—earth, fire, water, and wind—seem to be important symbols in traditional Japanese art forms as well as in your own quilt stories. Could you tell me about this?

Kumiko Sudo: Earth represents the universe and nature. Fire is a point of contact between gods and the people. Fire is used in various ways in Buddhist temples. Water represents the source of life—rainwater from the heavens for creatures on the earth; seawater for fish and shellfish. Gods are believed to live in water, and so water is worshipped. Wind symbolizes rulers and courageous warriors. This is because winds have such perfect freedom to blow east, west, north, and south. The Chinese character for the wind can sometimes be seen on walls as a wish for peace.

Penny McMorris: You often design with overlapping planes. In your quilt Picture Scrolls *(page 37), for example, you show the robes and hair of the two seated figures as a series of overlapping planes. I find that a particularly Japanese way of depicting three-dimensional space. Could you tell me about this?*

Kumiko Sudo: In the old picture scrolls of the nobility in the Heian Period, the viewpoint is from up above—a bird's-eye view. My quilt, *Picture Scrolls,* uses the same three-dimensional spatial perspective. There is a partition in front of some pillars, and a *kimono* in front of the partition. The *kimono* pieces are pieced in twenty overlapping planes to create a feeling of volume and depth.

Penny McMorris: The Japanese art form that had the most immediate and strongest influence on European and American artists was the woodblock print of the 1800s. Do these prints have a strong influence on your own work?

Kumiko Sudo: Hokusai, Hiroshige, Utamaro—they are my teachers. They continually teach me all kinds of lessons. The way Hokusai used blue, and the way Hiroshige used blue and red by gradating those colors always stays in my mind, the way they both balanced red with blue, their use of shadow, Utamaro's flawless sense of balance in his pictures of women with layered kimono sleeves and collars. I can always learn something from the work of these great artists.

Penny McMorris: Tell me about the strong contrasts in your work—you often seem to balance two opposites: heat and cold, curved lines and straight, light colors and dark, earth and sky. Can you talk about this?

Kumiko Sudo: I express my feelings with curved and straight lines as well as coordinated and balanced colors. I want my compositions to have a great harmony in the way the colors and lines all mingle together. In *Awakening* (page 31), I express the beam of hope, which springs eternal, and show it as a feeling that flies into the endless universe. On the other hand, in *Lady Kaguya* (page 33) the viewpoint moves in the opposite direction, from high up above, looking down. In *Sacred Horse* (page 43), the lines and colors express the joy of running. In *Ceremonial Bonfire* (page 49), I use black and red running and whirling through a statue of Buddha to symbolize the escape from struggle. *Fly, Cranes, Fly!* (page 53) shows cranes rapidly soaring into the endless sky. The names of my quilts naturally contain all of my thoughts and feelings at the time the quilt was being made.

Penny McMorris: This book combines some of your early quilts with your most recent work. When you look at your work as a whole, what strikes you about it?

Kumiko Sudo: I see how my work was influenced by every experience I have lived through. As drops of water falling on a rock carve a little hole in it, so, too, does every experience I have gone through, from the time I was conceived up until now, form my body of work.

Penny McMorris is vice president of the quilt design software firm The Electric Quilt Company and an art consultant specializing in contemporary quilts. She served as the corporate art curator for Owens Corning Corporation for twenty years. McMorris coauthored *The Art Quilt*, wrote *Crazy Quilts*, and has hosted thirty-six PBS television programs on quilting.

How to Use This Book

In this book you will find twenty-one original quilts inspired by scenes from Japan. Each sensational quilt is pictured, along with photographic details that emphasize the use of brilliant color combinations celebrating the passionate nature and the artistic sensibilities of Japanese culture.

You will also find complete patterns with instructions for making seven beautiful miniature quilts that capture 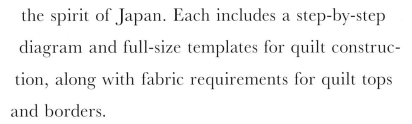 the spirit of Japan. Each includes a step-by-step diagram and full-size templates for quilt construction, along with fabric requirements for quilt tops and borders.

Each quilt is accompanied by a short story by Kumiko Sudo that helps us step inside Japanese history and culture, while creating a poetic ambience for the quilt.

Where to Begin

If you have made quilts from Kumiko Sudo's books *East Quilts West* or *East Quilts West II*, you will already be familiar with her use of color and some of her construction techniques. If you are new to Kumiko's

work, you will immediately notice that *Harmonies &*
Hurricanes is not like other quilting books. The designs,
the colors, the fabrics all come together in a unique
blending of Eastern and Western cultures. As you are
reading, why not try to create an atmosphere that will
help you understand a little more about Kumiko's cultural
heritage? Play some Japanese music in the background.
Sip a cup of green tea. Read the stories that tell you
about each of the quilt designs before you decide which
ones to make. All of these suggestions can help you feel at
ease and enter into the spirit of Kumiko's quilts.

For the quilts in *Harmonies & Hurricanes,* Kumiko used
silk from antique Japanese *kimonos* and *obi.* The seven
patterns can easily be made up in contemporary fabrics,
with an overall effect that still reflects a Japanese sensi-
bility. If you wish, you can probably duplicate
Kumiko's color choices. However, Kumiko feels that
color is an individual expression, and her selections
are intended for inspiration, not for instruction. In
Japan, certain colors and design patterns have
symbolic meaning. This is just one way in which

藤原敏行朝臣
住の江の岸による波よるさへや夢のかよひ路人目よくらむ

あはれとも
いふべき人は
思ほえで
身のいたづらに
なりぬべきかな

謙德公

Kumiko's cultural heritage has influenced her work, giving her quilts their unique character.

Pointers on Technique

Harmonies & Hurricanes differs from other quilting books not only in design and spirit but in technical matters, too. To ensure successful and enjoyable quilt making, keep these points in mind:

- *Harmonies & Hurricanes* is intended for people who have at least basic skills in sewing, appliqué, and quilt making.

- In contrast to traditional American quilts, Kumiko's designs take a very bold and daring approach to color. To gain confidence in color use, pin a base fabric of your choice to the wall, then add small amounts of as many different fabrics as you wish until you achieve that harmony that is so distinctive of Kumiko's work. Do not be afraid of using colors or designs that at first seem out of place or that you would normally shy away from. These are often the colors that will set off the overall quilt design and bring a quilt to life. A guiding rule is to experiment.

- Experienced quilters should find the patterns easy. These are an excellent starting point for beginners who can then move on to creating freestyle quilts of their own using the same fabric selection and techniques.

- All of the designs use appliqué stitches. For perfect appliqué, Kumiko's technique involves placing a fabric piece, with the seam allowance folded under, on top of the background square; the piece is then blind-stitched—or, as Kumiko calls it, "invisible-stitched"—by hand. Kumiko stitches everything—curved and straight—by hand. She always uses light gray or light beige thread, no matter what color the fabric, as the stitches will be invisible. Although the results are excellent when sewn by machine, Kumiko prefers to sew by hand, as she feels that the hand is directed not only by the eye but by the heart. The machine puts a distance between her and her work.

- The fabric requirements for borders on the quilts are figured without piecing. Usually, Kumiko selects an entirely different fabric from those used in the quilt, giving the quilts the appearance of framed pictures. The borders are always straight-pieced, never mitered.

- Full-size templates for the seven miniature quilts are provided at the back of the book. All templates and measurements need to have a ¼″ (0.6 mm) seam allowance added.

- Instructions are given for making quilt tops and borders only. To finish your project, you will need to buy batting and backing fabric, assemble the layers, and quilt them together. Kumiko considers quilting to be an accent "rather than something to be seen all over the picture." In quilts used as wall hangings, such stitching will suffice. The seven miniatures have no quilting at all. However, quilts used as bedding will require more extensive quilting. Kumiko seldom draws a design, but usually quilts freestyle. She rarely uses thread to match the fabric—for example, she often uses purple thread for yellow fabric, and green for blue fabric—and may use two or three different thread colors in one quilt.

The Quilts

Oh the beautiful Tatsuta River!

The layers of burning red maple

leaves float on the water, changing

the scene as the stream flows.

What a heavenly sight!

A *waka* poem by Kumiko Sudo.
Inspired by *The Silvery Moon over
the River*, page 97.

Raging Sea

This is the first quilt I made in "the promised land." The two boats struggling against the storm symbolize my own inner strife: hope troubled by despair, prosperity in the face of ordeals as a result of my move from Japan to America as I left behind friends and family for a new life. Despite the thunderous night, I see a light beyond the dark clouds, encouraging me to be valiant against all odds.

Raging Sea, 1986
27" × 37" (69 cm × 94 cm)
Private collection

Awakening

The rays of the burning sun are about to awaken the earth. Blue, cold glaciers are starting to melt and water is running in every direction to form rivers, seas, and lakes. You can hear the cracking of plants and trees as they burst from the soil. All creatures are stirring to face the new world. I have expressed these vigorous movements in two dimensions by representing their three-dimensionality in a cubist manner and by observing this from a world of four dimensions.

Awakening, 1986
26" × 30" (66 cm × 76 cm)
Private collection

Lady Kaguya

Lady Kaguya, a legendary classic, is based on the differences of lightness and darkness, life and death, virtue and vice in the human world. Found by a woodman cutting in a bamboo copse, Lady Kaguya was surrounded by a silvery aura. She grew to great beauty and wisdom and was pursued by many noblemen. But, being of divine origin, she was soon ordered to return to Heaven by the supreme being. She ascended to Heaven clad in a beautiful gown on a night of a full moon and scattered clouds. Here I endeavored to catch a glimpse of the sorrow depicting the final Ascension to Heaven. In this instance, I chose to use a variety of warm-colored silk fabrics. I intentionally obscured most of Lady Kaguya's figure in clouds to leave much to the imagination of the viewer.

Lady Kaguya, 1986
37″ × 27″ (94 cm × 69 cm)
Private collection

Ladies in Waiting

The imperial court relocated from Nara to Kyoto in the year 794 and remained the capital of Japan for 1,100 years. This was a period of cultural growth in every direction. The most remarkable change of all was the adaptation of a syllabary simplifying Chinese characters to represent Japanese sounds. The world's first great novel was written during the Kyoto period by Lady Murasaki Shikibu. *The Tale of Genji*, featuring the sights, sounds, manners, and morals of court life, celebrated refinement and awareness of beauty, which eventually became the heritage of the nation. In this design I have tried to depict brilliant garments consisting of twelve layers of silk *kimonos* in purple, blue, and green. I emphasize the abstract, red-colored fabrics permitted only among the aristocracy. I am sure viewers will sense the rustling of heavy silk attire and the sounds of poetry recitations, laughter, and chattering voices at court.

Ladies in Waiting, 1986
37″ × 34″ (94 cm × 86 cm)
Private collection

Highly realistic historical paintings were the artistic hallmark of the Kamakura period (1185–1333), which were re-created in lengthy scrolls that unrolled from right to left. These narrative picture scrolls became the foundation of the true Japanese style of painting. Court life was the subject matter of these scrolls, which depicted the rise and fall of the aristocracy and the dramatic exploits of warriors. In abstract, I created a scene of two nobles, surrounded by silk-screen partitions and stretched draperies, passing time by playing cards. Their long, flowing black hair is tucked away in their beautiful attire, as was the custom of the period. By the age of twelve, it was usual for a noblewoman to let her hair grow until it was a just a little longer than her height.

Picture Scrolls, 1989
48½″ × 29½″ (123 cm × 75 cm)
Permanent collection of
The Museum of Art,
University of Oregon

古代裂更紗

Genroku Period

In 1603, the *shogun*, Tokugawa, moved to the new capital, Edo (Tokyo), with his thousands of retainers. He was followed by artisans, merchants, and servants to supply the needs of the affluent ruling class. Carpenters were brought by the hundreds to construct mansions for the 250 feudal lords ordered by the *shogun* to keep their families in Edo as hostages. Almost overnight, this small village became a megalopolis. *Samurai*, as well as rich merchants, enjoyed the luxuries of theatergoing, woodblock prints, and literature. With influences from outside Japan, such as the Netherlands, China, and Korea, they also absorbed foreign aspects of culture. At that time the pleasure of cherry blossoms viewing was an important part of Japanese life. Here I lay out the elements of everyday life in juxtaposition and look back on them with nostalgia.

Genroku Period, 1986
27" × 32" (69 cm × 81 cm)
Private collection

Kabuki

As there is Shakespearean theater in England, so there is in Japan the unique tradition of *Kabuki* theater, which dates back more than 300 years. *Kabuki* is played only by male actors, many playing women's roles. They are accompanied onstage by black-robed assistants. I structure a *Kabuki* theater so that a passageway connects the main stage with the seats in the audience, enhancing an aspect important to *Kabuki,* the unity of the actors and audience. The movable scenery, special lighting effects, and use of theatrical illusion make possible the staging of fires, hurricanes, and snowstorms. Here I tried to convey the dramatic movement of the magnificent stage action and the beautiful colored costumes by manipulating various lines and circles.

Kabuki, 1987
32½" × 28" (83 cm × 71 cm)
Private collection

Sacred Horse

In the early 1500s there began a period of strife among the warlords of Japan as they constantly struggled for supreme power. After about a hundred years of fighting, one warrior, Tokugawa, became the nation's controlling regent. It was customary for the victorious clan to offer or dedicate a horse to the family shrine. In this composition I depicted the sacred horse, along with many battlefield flags. I placed the horse and flags diagonally in all directions and used a variety of striped fabrics to convey the high drama of the ceremony. I also used small and large circles and curved lines to express movement, fluidity, and the powerful spirit of the horse, which I tried to make as elegant and beautiful as possible by scattering florals on its torso and even its blinders. For the center of one flag, I designed a carriage wheel with ocean waves.

Sacred Horse, 1988
32″ × 47″ (81 cm × 119 cm)
Private collection

Zen

The *samurai* warriors were dedicated, even to death, to the defense of their master and his honor. They lived a life of frugality and discipline, of loyalty to the clan. Yet, caught in an endless period of war and turbulence in which family clans fought for local supremacy, a rare *samurai* might renounce these hardships. Secluding himself from society, he would become a Zen monk, laying down his sword and clothing himself in a simple *kimono* and straw hat. Here I show the monk's brilliant past life in many colors, in contrast to his later plain and simple life, in which he would walk from house to house playing the flute for small gifts of money or food. In the upper right-hand corner is the straw hat of a Zen monk; to the left is a piece of material, gold at the center, inscribed with Chinese characters. A monk would wear this on his surplice to keep away evil spirits. A small Chinese character on the orange background is meant to be incense. A dark-colored ribbon tied in a strong knot symbolizes the monk's determination to follow the path of Zen.

Zen, 1987
29½″ × 34″ (75 cm × 86 cm)
Private collection

The Great Buddha

Emperor Shomu decreed that each province should build a pagoda and a temple. The emperor himself had a fifty-three-foot statue of Daibutsu (Great Buddha) erected that towered over all others in the nation. The design we see here is an abstract presentation of Buddha sitting on a lotus flower. The gold shape with the white center in the center of the quilt is the spiritual eye of Buddhism, and the three rings on both sides are Buddha's hands. Buddha is always enshrined on the lotus flower, because the lotus flower opens in the morning with the first rays of sunlight, and it has many seeds with which to propagate throughout the world. The blue mazelike shapes surrounding Buddha at the center represent a priest's outer garment; they also symbolize a road map to heaven and suggest the different levels of the spiritual world.

The Great Buddha, 1987
31½" × 40" (80 cm × 102 cm)
Private collection

Ceremonial Bonfire

I n temples all over the country, the Japanese perform an annual event celebrating the belief that the spirits of their ancestors visit the earth. A large bonfire is built in front of the temple's gate as a guide or landmark for the visiting spirits. On this special day, the temple priests wear beautiful long robes. I have tried to bridge the two worlds of the spiritual and the material by using the long, curved lines of their robes. Within this ceremonial bonfire, I scattered several different shades of black, which represent the robes of temple priests; the blue colors are the quiet areas within each temple. The dominant color in this composition is orange, which represents the fire of the human spirit.

Ceremonial Bonfire, 1987
37" × 44½" (94 cm × 113 cm)
Private collection

Missionaries from the South

In 1543, a large, strange-looking ship appeared at the southern island of Tanegashima, and hundreds of men who wore baggy pants and short jackets disembarked. A Chinese man who accompanied them explained that they were Portuguese and that their purpose was trading goods and spreading Christianity. Within ten years, despite continuous opposition by Buddhist and Shinto priests, the missionaries built 200 churches and converted 150,000 Buddhists to Christianity, including high-ranking lords and their families. They brought such items from their home country as clocks, spectacles, and goblets as well as firearms. In this composition, I depicted in a very representational way four Portuguese men striding along the street in the foreground. Beneath the

Missionaries from the South, 1987
50" × 49½" (127 cm × 126 cm)
Private collection

beautiful stained glass at the top of the quilt, a noblewoman in the background proudly wears a cross around her neck.

Fly, Cranes, Fly!

In Japan, cranes are regarded as symbols of longevity. Using white and black as two dominant colors—one is the lightest of the light, the other the darkest of the dark—I adopted a bird's-eye view featuring two cranes ascending high into the sky. The sewing process required many varieties of white silk of differing values, brightness, and textures to heighten the birds' three-dimensional character. To achieve a degree of realism, I added red, blue, and green fabric between the white feathers to accentuate their individuality. On the black crane, I used a technique of brush painting in patching together blotched black fabrics with some pure colors, the latter being used as accents to capture the liveliness of the birds. The black borders, embellished with a silver crane design, create depth and distance, while blue and orange clouds extend the vastness of the sky.

Fly, Cranes, Fly!, 1987
40" × 46" (102 cm × 117 cm)
Private collection

Noh Play

N*oh* is a form of traditional Japanese theater, but in contrast to the realism of *Kabuki*, the *Noh* play possesses the austerity and understatement of religious drama. It is a theater of suggestion in which meaning is implied rather than stated. Different types of masks are used to represent various types of people. The stage design is extremely simple, and the use of props is kept to a minimum, while the costumes are extraordinarily beautiful and dignified. On the stage, a simple fan is the only instrument actors may use to help them express emotions. In this composition, repeated use of the fan shape is meant to express harmony among the characters. Straight lines and triangles are used to emphasize the curved figures.

Noh Play, 1987
39" × 46½" (99 cm × 118 cm)
Private collection

Kimono

Kimono, 1988
26″ × 38″ (66 cm × 97 cm)
*Permanent collection of the
Museum of American Folk Art,
New York*

Arevolution occurred in the arts in the late 1700s from which blossomed new types of literature, poetry, and fine arts. The turn of the century also saw the evolution of *Kabuki* theater from simple dancing to dramatic plays. This renaissance in the arts, the Genroku period, brought new and colorful designs to household decorations and clothing. The arts were no longer monopolized by the nobility but spread among ordinary citizens. To meet their demands, artisans were constantly changing the *kimono*'s color schemes, improving its quality, and creating innovative designs. Here I have depicted in an exaggerated manner a then-fashionable *kimono*, with long ribbons on the cuff and scattered layers of appliquéd flowers enhancing its beauty. A young girl dressed in her best offers a prayer, written on a small rectangular piece of paper, to a nearby shrine, as shown in the borders.

Temari

I remember as a child singing a song, *A Handball to the Lord,* and still find myself humming the tune. Though I do not recall all the lyrics, the song was about a handball that fell out of a child's hand and had to make a long journey home, encountering many different people, including a high-ranking lord. Unlike today's synthetic balls, the handball was handmade from cotton and silk threads and beautifully embroidered. As a child I imagined I was the handball, as I depicted in the design, and was flying free in the sky like a bird, making new friends and viewing the planets: Saturn, Venus, and Mars. Most of the fabrics used in this quilt were selected from children's *kimonos.* I hope someday to discover again those beautiful handballs in the sky.

Temari, 1988
34½" × 47" (88 cm × 119 cm)
Private collection

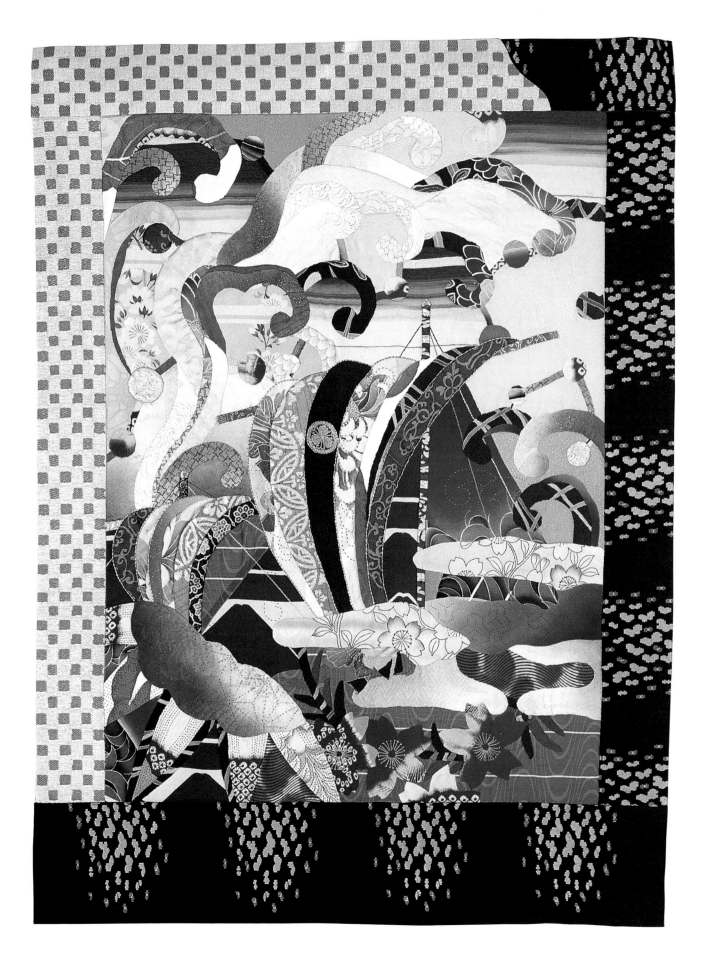

Homeward Bound

Customarily the first shipment of fresh vegetables and fish of the New Year was always treasured by the people of Japan; they called the ship carrying that cargo the *Takara Bune,* or treasure boat. In this joyful seascape, a treasure boat is about to anchor triumphantly at a hometown port laden with a large shipment. The cries of a high-spirited crew and the shouting and welcoming voices of families and friends fill the air in the small village. "Return home rich and successful," they say. This boat symbolizes a life itself, or parallels my own: I do not know when it may take place, but I certainly wish to meet again the ones I love most, accompanied by the sweetness of success. The rolling waves on the upper part of the quilt represent the obstacles in life, while bamboo leaves and flowers below symbolize happy occasions.

Homeward Bound, 1987
34½″ × 31½″ (88 cm × 80 cm)
Private collection

Poetry Party at Court

Poetry Party at Court, 1990
47″ × 37″ (119 cm × 94 cm)
Private collection

uring the Heian period, there was a gracious pastime that the aristocracy enjoyed called *Uta-awase*. The emperors, the nobles, and the poets gathered to write poems. The topics they chose—flowers, the changing of the seasons, and all kinds of creatures—conveyed the beauty of Heian people's hearts. In *The Tale of Genji*, the classic novel of the Heian period, the hero, Prince Genji, divided his palace into four to represent the four seasons, and housed his four beautiful wives in them. Imagine how he must have enjoyed the cherry blossoms in the Spring Palace or the fall colors in the Autumn Palace, where the *kimonos* of little children displayed pretty asters, bush clover, dianthus, and other lovely fall flowers. During the Edo period, one hundred poets selected poems from the *waka* poems of the Heian era and called the collection "Hundred People's Poems." Even to the present day, people read these poems at New Year. They have become an important part of Japanese literature.

Ukiyo-e

he celebrated painter Utamaro Kitagawa is the best
known of all *Ukiyo-e* artists. Utamaro was born in 1754
and devoted his life of fifty years to the art of *Ukiyo-e*,
"The Painting of the Floating World." He is most remembered for his paintings of courtly beauties, and his way of
drawing the necklines of ladies became a signature of his
work. Rather than depicting the nobles or *shoguns* in their
grand castles, he chose to express the simpler beauties of
daily life. This piece is influenced by the work of Utamaro.

Ukiyo-e, 1994
37" × 46½" (94 cm × 118 cm)
Private collection

An actress has just left the
stage and is standing by
the curtain fixing her
collar. To emphasize the
neckline, I arranged the
collar by layering fabrics
of different colors. With
this arrangement I wanted
to re-create the courtly
beauties of those days in
fabrics. The Chinese
characters represent the names of women who would have
been Utamaro's models.

Cherry Blossoms Viewing

Japan has four very distinct seasons. Each has its own poetic beauty that captures the hearts of the people. The viewing of the cherry blossoms each spring, enjoyed for more than a thousand years, is the tradition the Japanese love most. The people of the Heian period lived with nature, but brought to it an artistic interpretation of their own. Here, a high-ranking nobleman arranges a cherry blossoms viewing party for the

Cherry Blossoms Viewing, 1994
43" × 36" (109 cm × 91 cm)
Private collection

court ladies. At each side of the front of the palace, he carefully places blossomed cherry branches in porcelain vases. All over the garden, the lovely flowers bloom on the manicured trees. The young noblemen and their ladies gather in the garden in light, layered silk spring *kimonos.* The pink silks in the ladies' *kimonos* complement the pink of the blossoms as the delicate petals fall gently around them. The full cherry blossoms and the ladies' pink *kimonos* meet in the garden. The calming colors of nature and the artistry of the *kimonos* combine on this wonderful Heian spring day.

Five Beauties, Edo Period

About one thousand years ago, during the Heian Era, there was a great poet, Ono-no-Komachi, who was one of the *Rokkasen*, the six famous poets. Ono-no-Komachi, a very beautiful lady, was painted by the graceful brush of the celebrated *Ukiyo-e* artist Utamaro. This quilt is inspired by Utamaro's

Five Beauties, Edo Period, 1995
41″ × 37″ (104 cm × 94 cm)
Private collection

paintings of Ono-no-Komachi and other courtly beauties. On a lovely summer evening, the ladies chase fireflies on the bank of a stream. Their voices dance in the summer breeze as it catches the sleeves and collars of their *kimonos.* As reflected in this quilt, Utamaro's works had a significant influence on European impressionist artists when they were first seen in Europe in the eighteenth century.

The Patterns

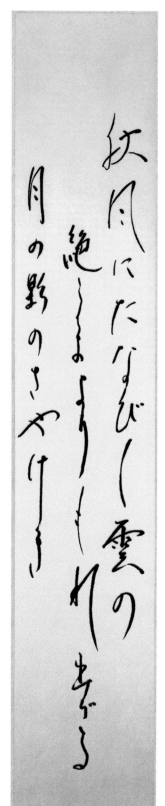

When the autumn wind blows,

the clouds trot across the moon.

The moon glows between them as

the clouds run around. What a

lovely party!

A *waka* poem by Kumiko Sudo.
Inspired by *Autumn Poetry*,
page 87.

Moonlit Night

One late summer evening, a full moon spread her light all around the garden of a palace. It was the night of the traditional moon-watching party, and tiny altars with rice cakes lay here and there around the garden. A mother, tears in her eyes, talked quietly to the moon. "Please tell me, how is my daughter whom you took from me so long ago? It is too many years since I last saw her, and I am sad without her." The moon, hearing her pleas, opened up a huge fan, made a silk pathway, and sent a beautiful lady in a gorgeous layered *kimono* to her mother. The mother was so happy that her tears were transformed into hundreds of pearls. The mother took one pearl for herself and handed the rest to her daughter. The daughter fluttered her *kimono* in the sky and set out on her journey back to the moon.

Making the Quilt

The mother watches the moon high above the gardens from the palace. Repeating the same fabric in the moon and in parts of the *kimono* unites the quilt and gives it balance. Arranging the same floral fabric on the left, off-center, and on the right strengthens this effect.

Moonlit Night, 1995
21½" × 16" (55 cm × 41 cm)

Moonlit Night

21½" × 16" (55 cm × 41 cm)

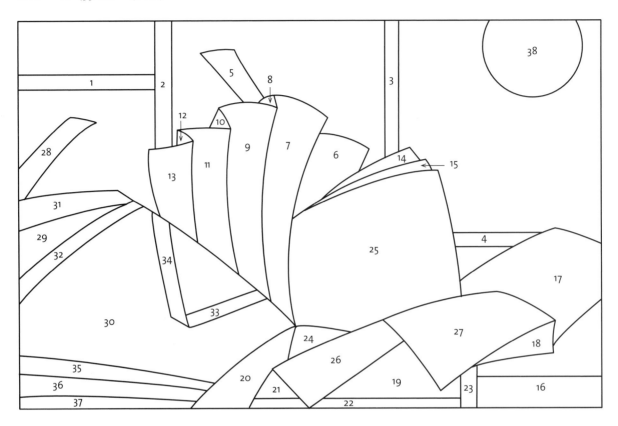

FABRIC REQUIREMENTS

Background fabric	½ yard (0.5 m)
Appliqué pieces	Small pieces of fabric scraps or purchase ⅛ yard (0.1 m) of various fabrics
Borders	½ yard (0.5 m)

CUTTING

Background	Cut one base rectangle 12" × 17½" (30.5 cm × 44.4 cm)
Appliqué pieces	Cut pieces, adding ¼" (0.6 cm) seam allowance to templates
Borders	Cut four strips 3" × 17½" (7.6 cm × 44.4 cm)

TO MAKE THE QUILT

Fold the background rectangle into fourths to make creases, then lay out all of the templates and draw guide lines.

1. Appliqué 1, 2, 3, 4, 5, 6, 16, 21, 22, 23, 28, and 38 onto the background fabric, leaving raw edges as shown.

2. Appliqué 7 onto 6. Appliqué 8 onto 7. Fold the dotted line 7 to the inside, then tack it. Leave it open.

3. Appliqué 9 onto 8 and 7.

4. Appliqué 10, 11, 12, and 13, in sequence, onto 9.

5. Appliqué 14 and 15 onto 3 and 6.

1.

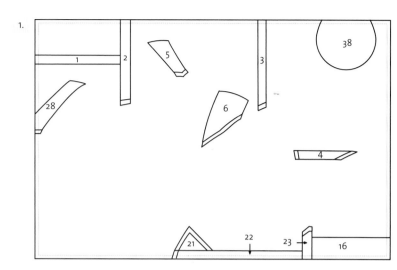

2.

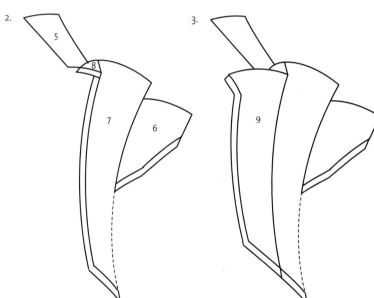

3.

4.

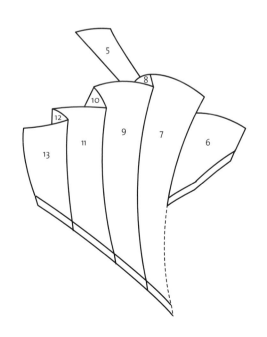

5.

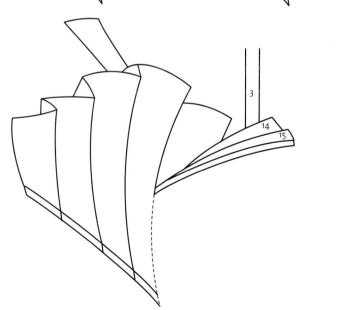

6.

7.

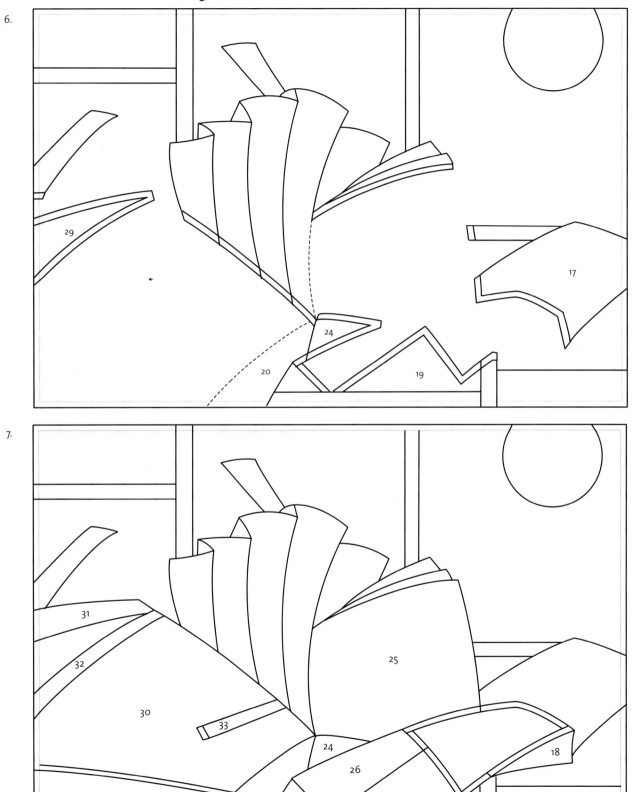

8.

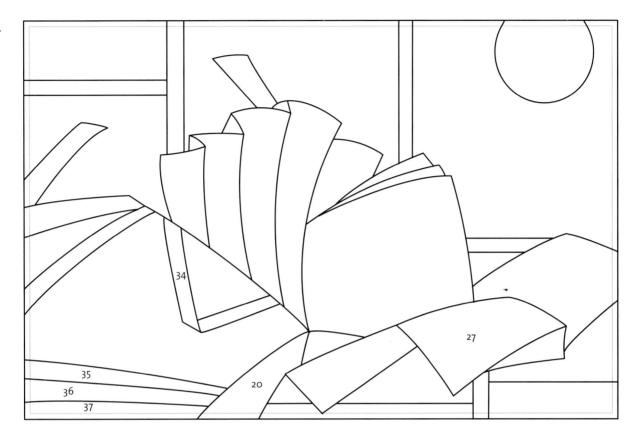

6. Appliqué 17, 19, 20, 24, and 29 onto the base fabric. Fold the dotted line 20 to the inside, then tack it. Leave it open.

7. Appliqué 18, 26, 25, 30, 31, 32, and 33, in sequence. Finish the appliqué on 7.

8. Appliqué 27 and 34, then 35, 36, and 37. Finish the appliqué on 20.

   Sew top and bottom borders, then sew side borders.

A Hamlet Among the Hills

About a thousand years ago, there was a nobleman of very high rank who was very tired of his busy town life and wanted to escape to the countryside. Leaving his wife and daughter behind, he took his favorite books, his *kimono*s, and a simple cane. He built a little hamlet in the mountains. The joy of his life was to watch the changing seasons, to see the wild azaleas, and to see the colors of sunset decorate the mountainsides. People from the village nearby thought him a fool for abandoning his rich lifestyle, but he would sit beneath the moon, his maple cane at his side, listening to the sounds of nature, and he would feel at peace.

Making the Quilt

By the light of a full moon, the mother and daughter gaze at the mountain range from their manor. Four red highlights, four floral fabrics, four burgundies, three checks, and two blues bring the moon into prominence while keeping the whole quilt in balance.

A Hamlet Among the Hills, 1996
21″ × 16″ (53 cm × 41 cm)

A Hamlet Among the Hills

21″ × 16″ (53 cm × 41 cm)

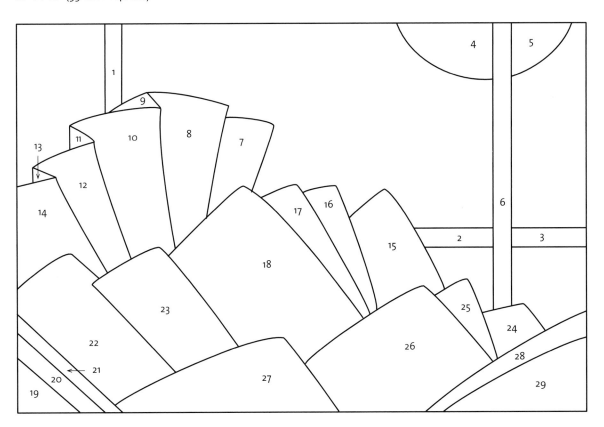

Fabric Requirements

Background fabric	½ yard (0.5 m)
Appliqué pieces	Small pieces of fabric scraps or purchase ⅛ yard (0.1 m) of various fabrics
Borders	½ yard (0.5 m)

Cutting

Background	Cut one base rectangle 12″ × 18″ (30.5 cm × 45.7 cm)
Appliqué pieces	Cut pieces, adding ¼″ (0.6 cm) seam allowance to templates
Borders	Cut four strips 3½″ × 18″ (8.9 cm × 45.7 cm)

To make the quilt

Fold the background rectangle into fourths to make creases, then lay out all of the templates and draw guide lines.

1. Appliqué 1, 2, 3, 4, 5, 6, 7, 15, 19, and 24 onto the background fabric, leaving raw edges as shown.

2. Appliqué 8 onto 7, then 16 onto 15.

3. Appliqué 9, 11, 10, 13, 12, and 14.

4. Appliqué 17, 18, and 23 onto 16. Leave open the dotted line on 23 after tacking.

5. Insert 22 under 23, then appliqué. Appliqué 25 and 26.

6. Appliqué 27, 28, 29, 20, and 21.

   Sew top and bottom borders, then sew side borders.

1.
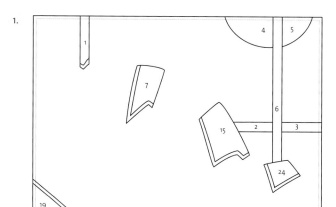
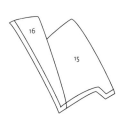

2.
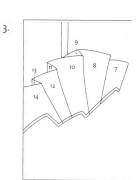

3.
4.

5.
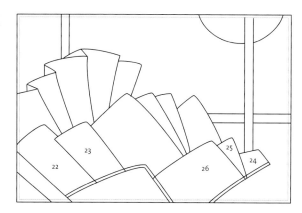

6.
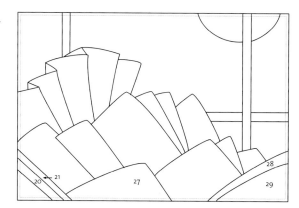

An Autumn Afternoon

Slowly summer passed, the hot sun shining against the mountains day after day. When the trees started putting on their autumn colors, an old lady visited the village where she had lived as a child. She remembered how she would play outside a cottage where fabric was made. When the autumn wind blew, the maple leaves would tumble down and dance to the sound of a wooden hammer, pounding on silk to make it shine. Every fall, she would feel melancholy for this sound in the autumn wind. Now, she was home again, the autumn colors and this beloved sound all around her. At her feet, wild chrysanthemums bloomed, taking the old lady back to those lost days.

Making the Quilt

As early as the Heian period, checks, or *ichimatsu*, were a popular design. Later, during the Edo period, *ichimatsu* was one of the most well-known and best loved of all Japanese designs.

An Autumn Afternoon, 1993
23" × 17" (58 cm × 43 cm)

An Autumn Afternoon

23″ × 17″ (58 cm × 43 cm)

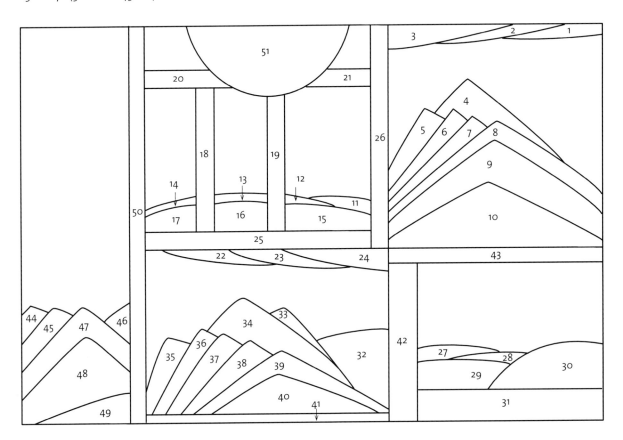

Fabric Requirements

Background fabric ½ yard (0.5 m)

Appliqué pieces Small pieces of fabric scraps or purchase ⅛ yard (0.1 m) of various fabrics

Borders ½ yard (0.5 m)

Cutting

Background Cut one base rectangle 12″ × 18″ (30.5 cm × 45.7 cm)

Appliqué pieces Cut pieces, adding ¼″ (0.6 cm) seam allowance to templates

Borders Cut four strips 3½″ × 18″ (8.9 cm × 45.7 cm)

TO MAKE THE QUILT

Fold the background rectangle into fourths to make creases, then lay out all of the templates and draw guide lines.

1. Appliqué 1, 4, 11, 13, 14, 21, 22, 27, 32, 35, 44, and 46 onto the background fabric, leaving raw edges as shown.

2. Appliqué 12 onto 11. Appliqué 15, then 16 and 17 onto 13 and 14.

3. Appliqué 18, 19, 20, and 51.

4. Appliqué 2 and 3, in sequence, onto 1. Appliqué 5, 6, 7, 8, 9, and 10 onto 4.

5. Appliqué 23 and 24 onto 22. Appliqué 33, 34, 35, 36, 37, 38, 39, 40, and 41.

6. Appliqué 28, 29, 30, and 31 onto 27.

7. Appliqué 45, 47, 48, and 49 onto 44 and 46.

8. Appliqué 25, 26, 42, 43, and 50.

Sew top and bottom borders, then sew side borders.

1.
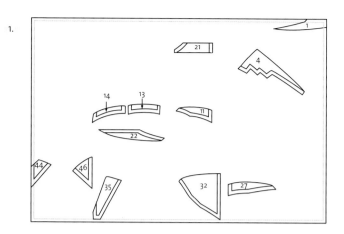

2.
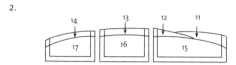

3.
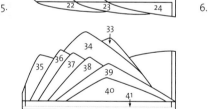

4.
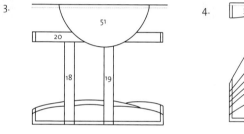

5.
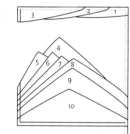

6.
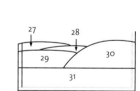

7.
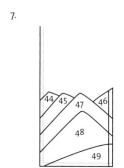

8.
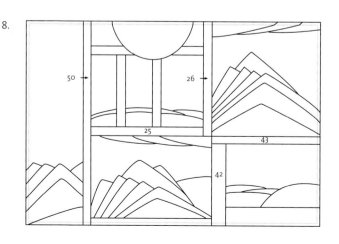

Autumn Poetry

During the Heian period, there lived a great poet in the city, who was admired for her writings on the gracious lifestyle of the nobility. A friend who was also a poet invited her to leave the city to live in a mountain hamlet and write poetry to nature. They stayed overnight at the cottage of a Buddhist priest, surrounded by a field of silver grass and trees. As they sat on the verandah in the early evening, the grasses moved in the autumn wind like ocean waves. The mountains beyond the field were already colored by the shadow of the evening. The two young poets wrote poem after poem. The lady was moved by the beauty of the nature and the magical atmosphere of the evening. The night passed quickly and the purple color of dawn chased the moon from the sky. Rice papers with their poems lay all around, stirring gently in the autumn wind.

Making the Quilt

The black lines are the branches of a plum tree, holding their beautiful flowers against the sky. The two red lines on the left enhance the pretty colors.

Autumn Poetry, 1986
24″ × 18″ (61 cm × 46 cm)

Autumn Poetry

24″ × 18″ (61 cm × 46 cm)

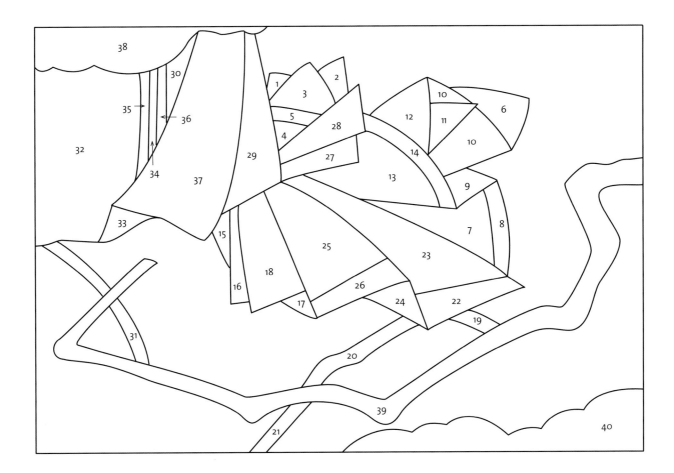

Fabric Requirements

Background fabric	½ yard (0.5 m)
Appliqué pieces	Small pieces of fabric scraps or purchase ⅛ yard (0.1 m) of various fabrics
Borders	½ yard (0.5 m)

Cutting

Background	Cut one base rectangle 12″ × 18″ (30.5 cm × 45.7 cm)
Appliqué pieces	Cut pieces, adding ¼″ (0.6 cm) seam allowance to template
Borders	Cut four strips 3½″ × 18″ (8.9 cm × 45.7 cm)

TO MAKE THE QUILT

Fold the background rectangle into fourths to make creases, then lay out all of the templates and draw guide lines.

1. Appliqué 1, 2, 4, 6, 7, 15, 17, 19, 20, 21, 31, and 40 onto the background fabric, leaving raw edges as shown.

2. Appliqué 39 onto 19, 20, 21, and 31.

   Appliqué 16 onto 15, then 18 onto 17.

   Appliqué 3 and 5 onto 1, 2, and 4.

   Appliqué 8, 9, 10, 11, 12, and 13. Appliqué 14.

3. Appliqué 22, 23, 24, 25, and 26.

   Appliqué 27 and 28.

4. Appliqué 29, 30, 32, 33, 35, 34, 27, and 36, in that order.

   Appliqué 37, then 38.

   Sew top and bottom borders, then sew side borders.

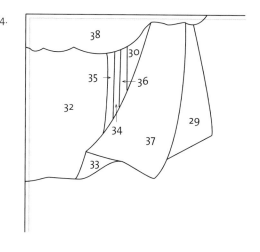

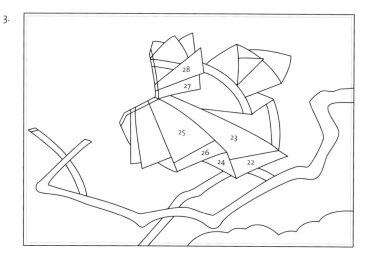

Ladies in a Fine Snow

Aprincess travelling to the capital, Kyoto, to be married thought with sadness of the beloved flower garden she had left behind. As her carriage arrived at the mansion where she was to stay, the princess was delighted to see many new and unusual flowers. Among them were brilliant red blossoms, such as she had never seen before. At dinner, she found three of those beautiful camellias on her tray. That night, in the cool spring breeze, the princess fell into a deep sleep. Feeling a light on her cheek and thinking it was moonlight, she awoke and opened a little window by her bedside. Outside, she saw a silver bright world of fresh-fallen snow covering the garden. Bright camellias, peeking out their pretty little red faces here and there, welcomed the princess to her new life.

Making the Quilt

This composition is inspired by the designs of Heian picture scrolls, where scenes are viewed from afar or from above, without walls, doors, or ceilings. Here, we look inside a room from above. The black lines are the posts of the room.

Ladies in a Fine Snow, 1993
22″ × 16″ (56 cm × 41 cm)

Ladies in a Fine Snow

22″ × 16″ (56 cm × 41 cm)

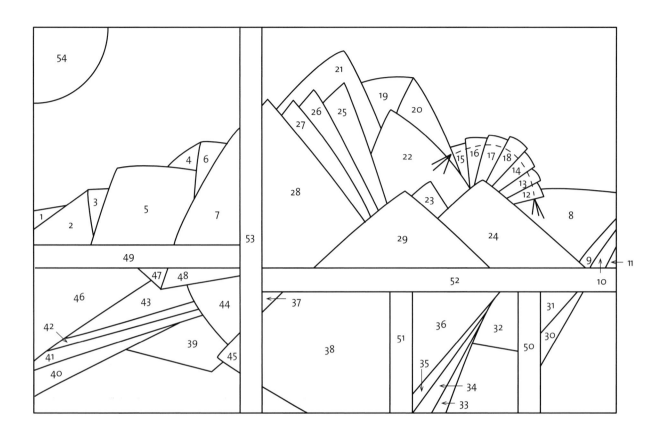

FABRIC REQUIREMENTS

Background fabric	½ yard (0.5 m)
Appliqué pieces	Small pieces of fabric scraps, or purchase ⅛ yard (0.1 m) of various fabrics
Borders	½ yard (0.5 m)

CUTTING

Background	Cut one base rectangle 12″ × 18″ (30.5 cm × 45.7 cm)
Appliqué pieces	Cut pieces, adding ¼″ (0.6 cm) seam allowance to templates
Borders	Cut two strips 3″ × 12″ (7.6 cm × 30.5 cm) Cut two strips 3″ × 22½″ (7.6 cm × 57 cm)

To make the quilt

Fold the background rectangle into fourths to make creases, then lay out all of the templates and draw guide lines.

1. Appliqué 1, 8, 19, 30, 32, 37, 39, and 54 onto the background fabric, leaving raw edges as shown.

2. Appliqué 2, 3, 4, 5, 6, and 7, in sequence.

3. Appliqué 21 onto 19, then 11, 10, 9, and 12 onto 8. Appliqué 13 and 14 onto 12, then appliqué 16 and 17 onto 15.

1.

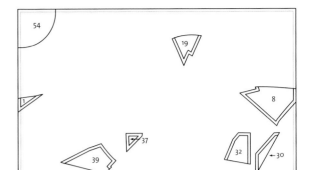

2.

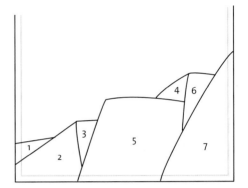

3.

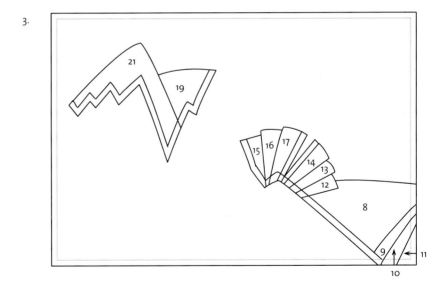

4.

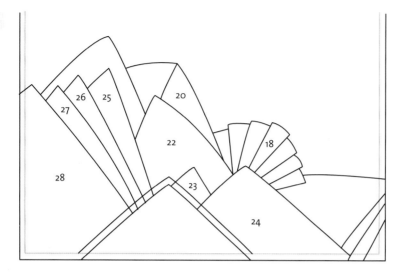

5.

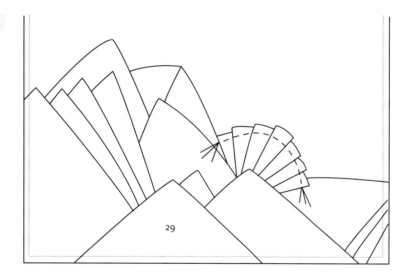

6.

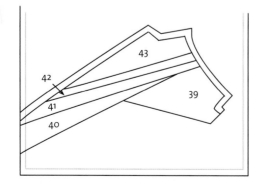

7.

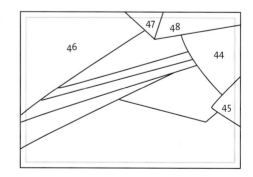

4. Appliqué 18 onto 14, then onto 17, 20 onto 19 and 15.

   Appliqué 22, 23, and 24 onto 21, then 25, 26, 27, and 28 onto 22 and 21.

5. Appliqué 29. Sew a running stitch and tassels on each end along fan.

6. Appliqué 40, 41, 42, and 43 onto 39.

7. Appliqué 44, 45, 46, 47, and 48 onto 43.

8. Appliqué 38 onto 37.

9. Appliqué 33, 34, 35, and 36 onto 32.

10. Appliqué 31 onto 30.

11. Appliqué the strips 49, 50, 51, 52, and 53.

    Sew side borders, then sew top and bottom borders.

8.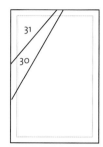

9.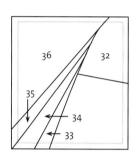

10.

11.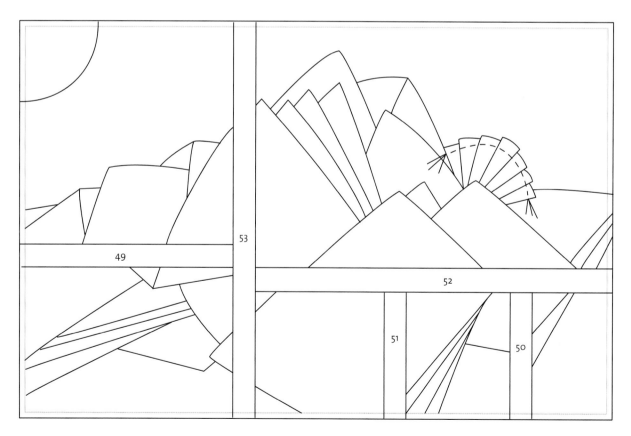

The Silvery Moon over the River

I n the early late winter evening, a warrior was on a journey through the mountains to the capital. The snow fell deep and soft around him, day after day. The silver winter moonlight, reflecting on a river, led the warrior on his way. As he walked, the warrior asked the moon to lead him safely to his daughter's home. Then the moon sent a silver cotton cloud that took him to the golden palace in the twinkling of an eye. There in the silver moonlight, the warrior saw his beautiful child before him. The moon, looking at the scene, left his silver tears and golden smile and went home.

Making the Quilt

A beautiful *kimono* is spread out beneath the brilliant silver moon. Picture the layers of the *kimono* also as a mountain range, bringing the moon into prominence.

The Silvery Moon over the River, 1994
23" × 17" (56 cm × 43 cm)

The Silvery Moon over the River

23" × 17" (58 cm × 43 cm)

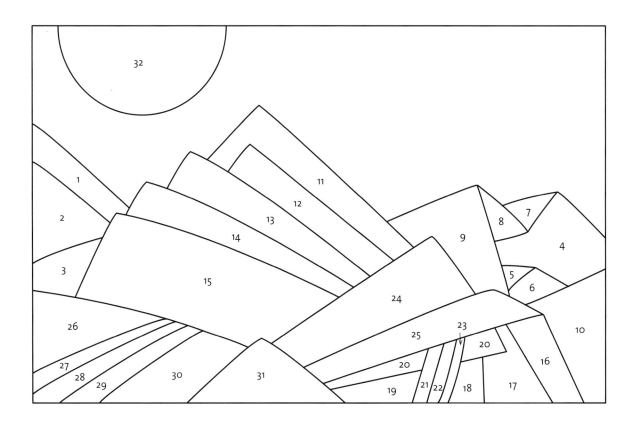

Fabric Requirements

Background fabric	½ yard (0.5 m)
Appliqué pieces	Small pieces of fabric scraps, or purchase ⅛ yard (0.1 m) of various fabrics
Borders	½ yard (0.5 m)

Cutting

Background	Cut one base rectangle 12" × 18" (30.5 cm × 45.7 cm)
Appliqué pieces	Cut pieces, adding ¼" (0.6 cm) seam allowance to templates
Borders	Cut four strips 3½" × 18" (8.9 cm × 45.7 cm)

To make the quilt

Fold the background rectangle into fourths to make creases, then lay out all of the templates and draw guide lines.

1. Appliqué 1 and 4 onto the background fabric, leaving raw edges as shown.

2. Appliqué 2 and 3 onto 1.

3. Appliqué 5 and 7 onto 4, then 6 and 8.

4. Appliqué 9 and 10.

5. Appliqué 11, 12, 13, 14, and 15, then 16 and 26.

6. Appliqué 17, 18, 19, 20, and 24, then 27, 28, 29, and 30. Appliqué 25, 31, 32.

7. Appliqué 21, 22, 23.

Sew top and bottom borders, then sew side borders.

1.

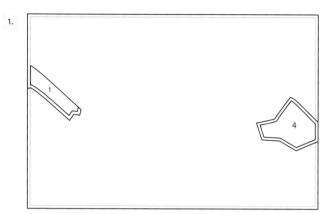

2.

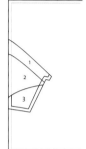

3.

4.

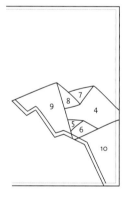

5.

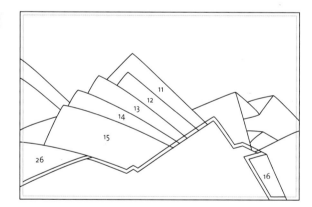

6.

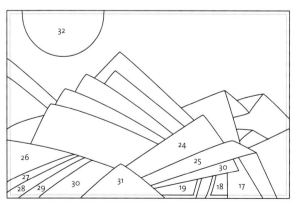

7.

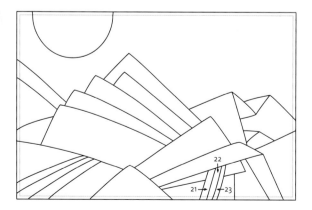

An Old Ruin

About a thousand years ago, in the time of a powerful aristocracy, there lived a beautiful maiden. She enjoyed a life of luxury and pleasure, living in a grand palace, surrounded by flowers, with her many maids. She dressed in gorgeous *kimonos* and passed her days writing poetry. She was admired by all who saw her. But times changed, and the powers of the *samurai* grew stronger than those of the nobility. Noble families disappeared; once-great lords retreated to the Buddhist temples. What happened to that beautiful noble maiden? She, too, was gone, a memory of better times. A priest who had once known her visited her now-ruined palace, the tiles fallen and the weeds overgrowing the flowers. He sighed sadly and said, "It sends a spear through my heart to see the dead grass and the shadows of her beautiful silk *kimono*. How vain is prosperity in life, and how easily is it defeated!"

Making the Quilt

Picture the exiled noble ladies of the Heian period on a boat in the middle of a blue-green ocean. The red posts of the boat reflect the sunset that implies the fall of the nobility.

An Old Ruin, 1997
21½" × 16" (55 cm × 41 cm)

An Old Ruin

21½ ″ × 16″ (55 cm × 41 cm)

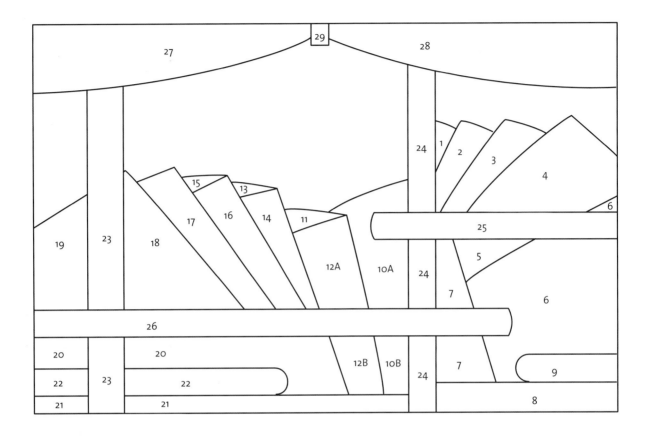

FABRIC REQUIREMENTS

Background fabric	½ yard (0.5 m)
Appliqué pieces	Small pieces of fabric scraps, or purchase ⅛ yard (0.1 m) of various fabrics
Borders	½ yard (0.5 m)

CUTTING

Background	Cut one base rectangle 12″ × 17½″ (30.5 cm × 44.4 cm)
Appliqué pieces	Cut pieces, adding ¼″ (0.6 cm) seam allowance to templates
Borders	Cut two strips 3″ × 12″ (7.6 cm × 30.5 cm) Cut two strips 3″ × 23″ (7.6 cm × 58.4 cm)

To make the quilt

Fold the background rectangle into fourths to make creases, then lay out all of the templates and draw guide lines.

1. Appliqué 1, 5, 10A, 19, and 20 onto the background fabric, leaving raw edges as shown.

2. Appliqué 11, 12A, 13, 14, 15, 16, 17, and 18, in sequence, onto 10A.

3. Appliqué 12B onto 10B and 20, then appliqué 22 and 21 onto 20.

4. Appliqué 2, 3, and 4, in sequence, onto 1.

   Appliqué 6 onto 4 and 5, then appliqué 7 and 8.

5. Appliqué 9, 23, 24, 25, and 26.

   Appliqué 27, 28, and 29.

   Sew side borders, then sew top and bottom borders.

   If desired, attach tassels to each side of block as shown in photograph.

1.
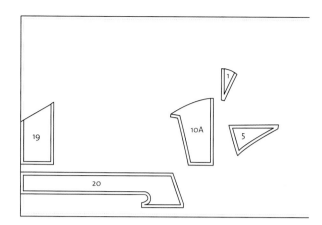

2.
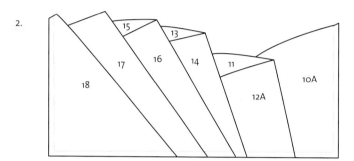

3.
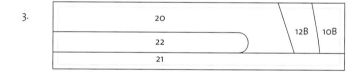

4.
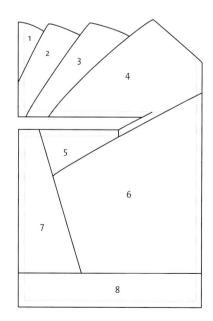

5.
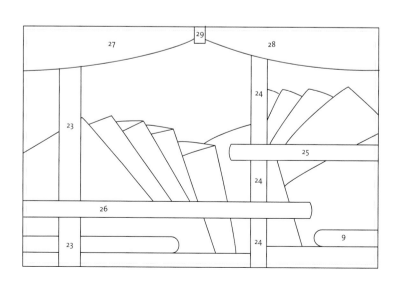

Templates

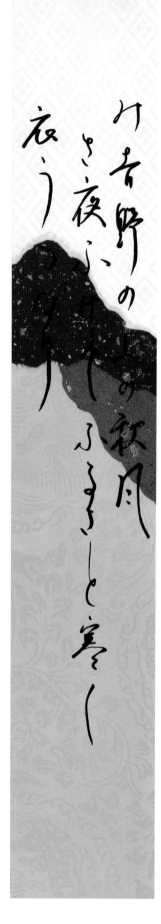

Traveling to the old capital, Yamoto, I stayed overnight at the village of Yoshino. Thinking I saw the beautiful moonlight, I opened a window in the darkness before dawn. My, it was not the moon, but the snow that fell during the night, sparkling in the dark over the hills and dales.

A *waka* poem by Kumiko Sudo.
Inspired by *An Autumn Afternoon*,
page 83.

Moonlit Night

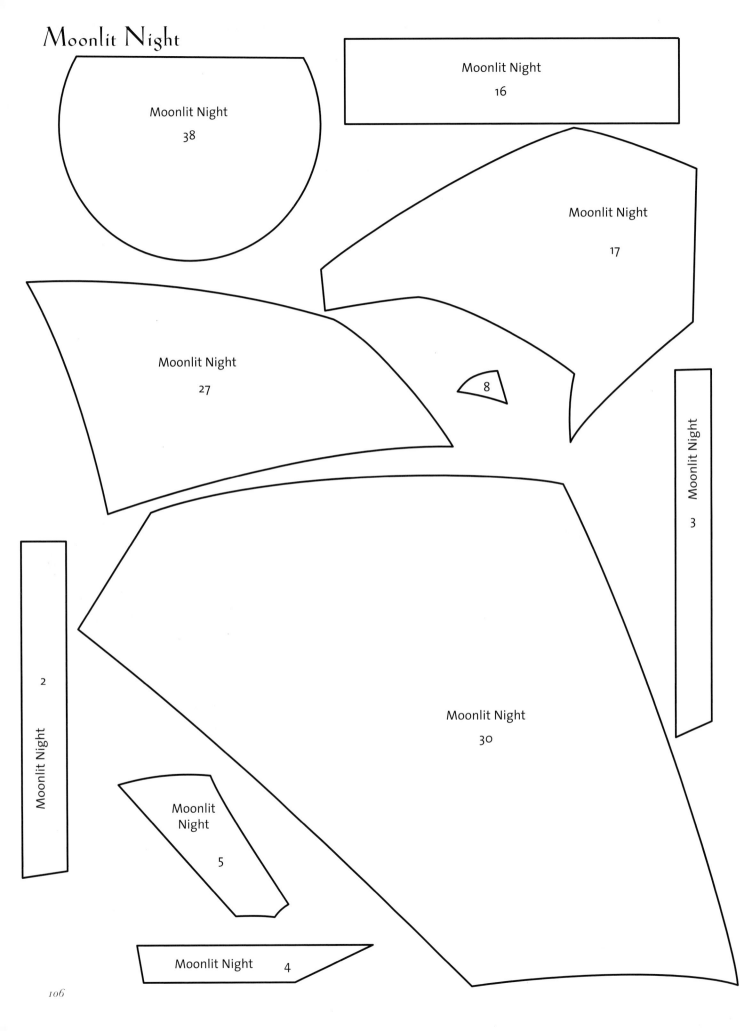

Moonlit Night

38

Moonlit Night

16

Moonlit Night

17

Moonlit Night

27

8

Moonlit Night

3

Moonlit Night

2

Moonlit Night

30

Moonlit
Night

5

Moonlit Night   4

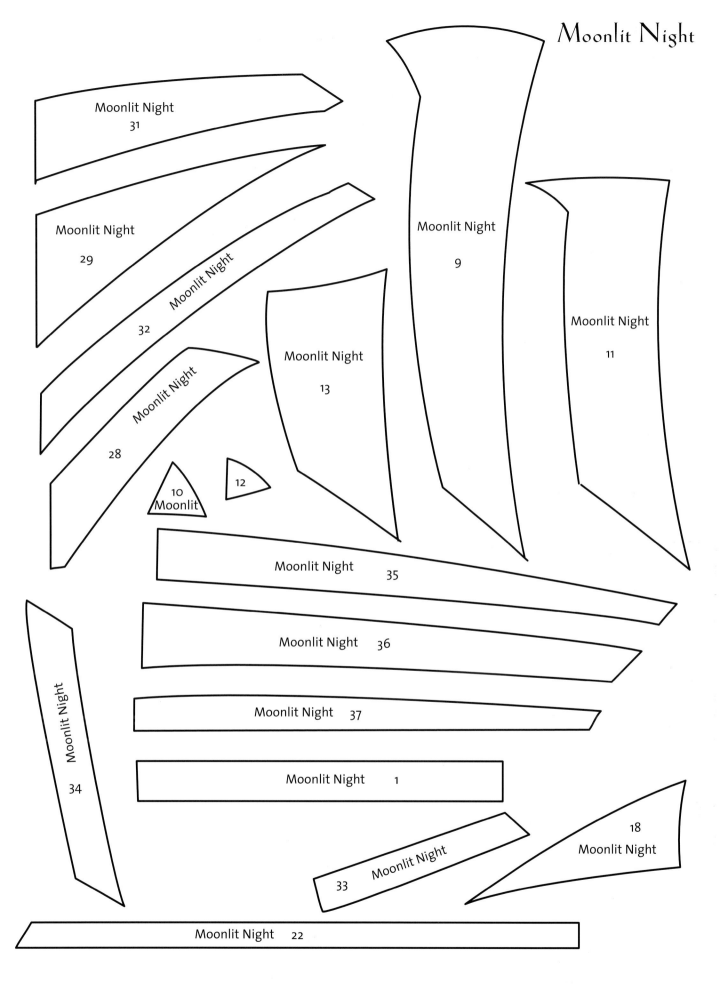

Moonlit Night

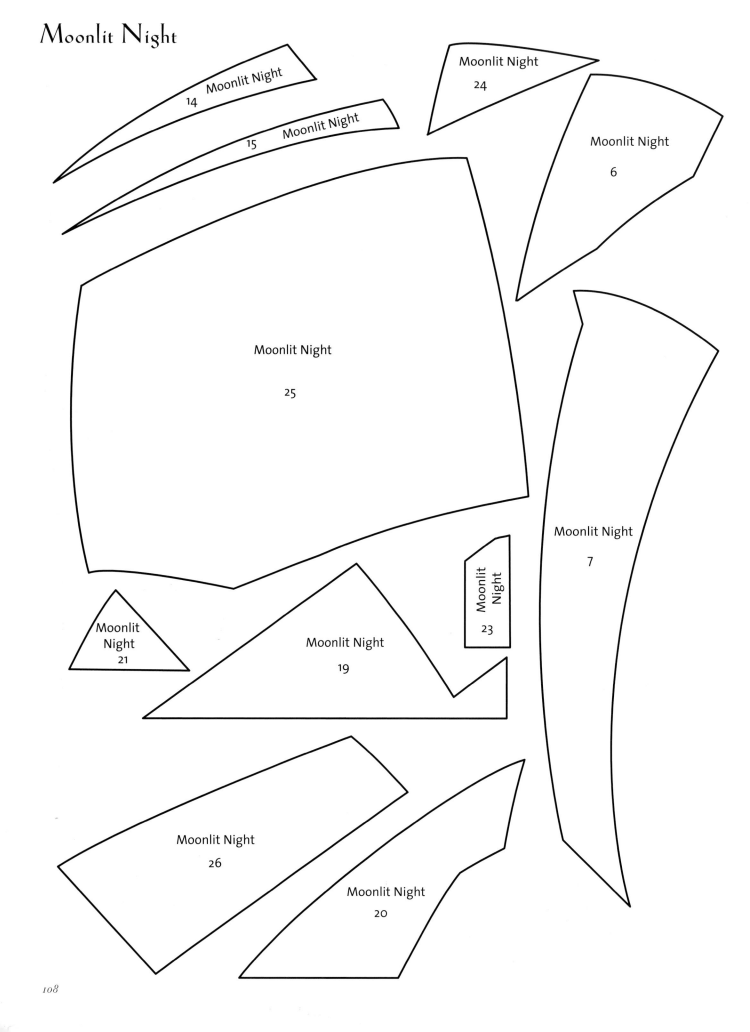

Moonlit Night
14

Moonlit Night
15

Moonlit Night
24

Moonlit Night
6

Moonlit Night
25

Moonlit Night
7

Moonlit Night
21

Moonlit Night
19

Moonlit Night
23

Moonlit Night
26

Moonlit Night
20

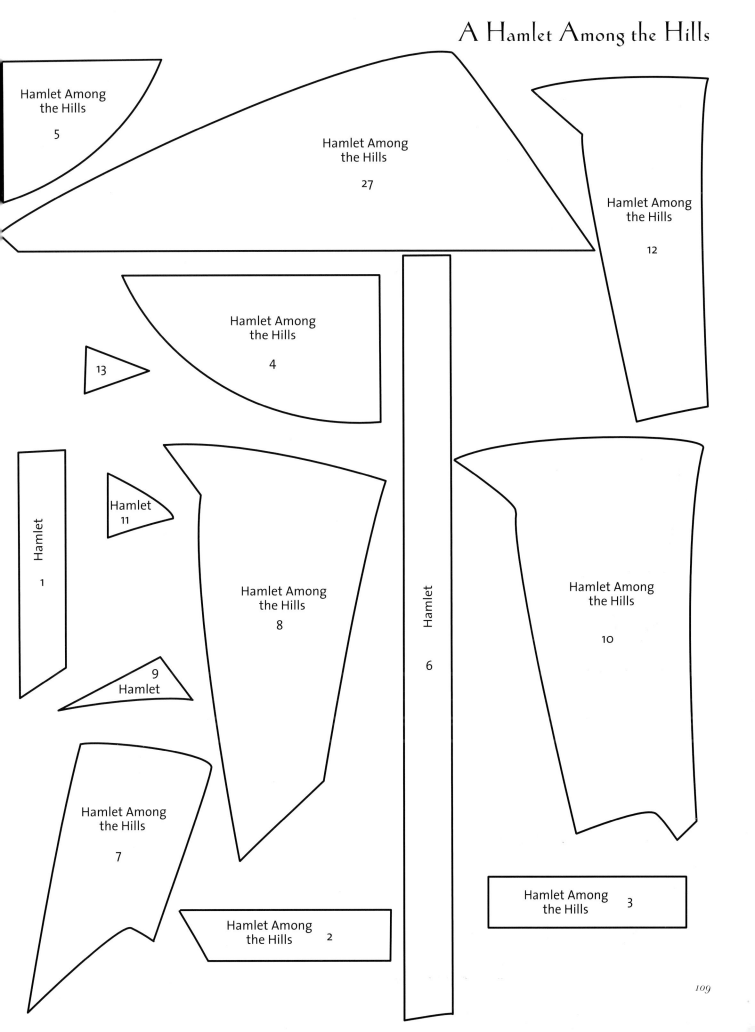

A Hamlet Among the Hills

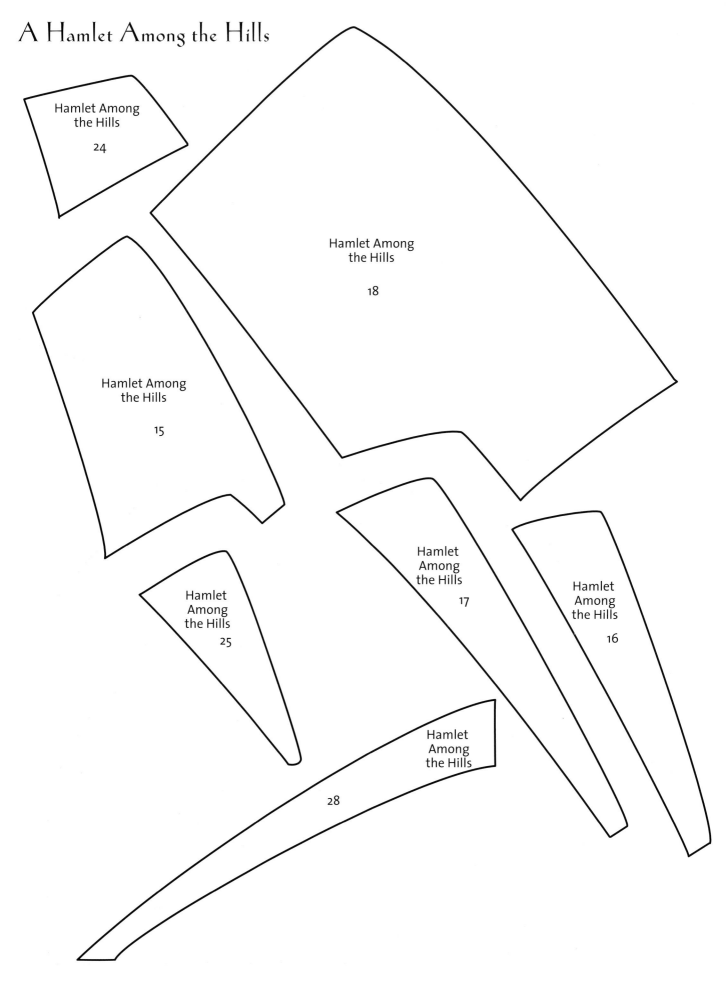

Hamlet Among the Hills

24

Hamlet Among
the Hills

18

Hamlet Among
the Hills

15

Hamlet
Among
the Hills

25

Hamlet
Among
the Hills

17

Hamlet
Among
the Hills

16

Hamlet
Among
the Hills

28

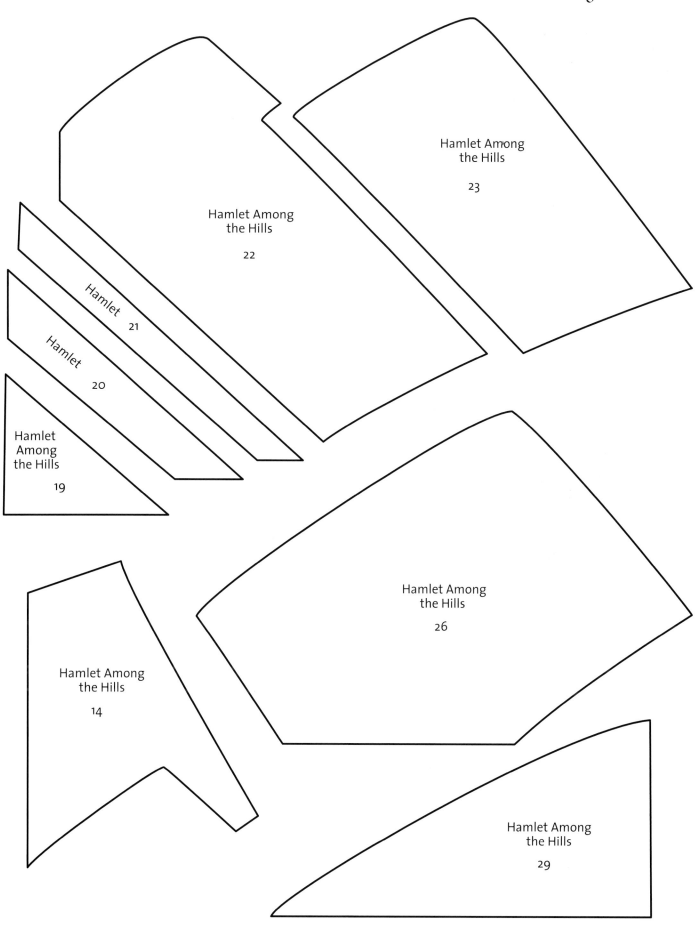

Hamlet Among
the Hills

23

Hamlet Among
the Hills

22

Hamlet
21

Hamlet
20

Hamlet
Among
the Hills

19

Hamlet Among
the Hills

26

Hamlet Among
the Hills

14

Hamlet Among
the Hills

29

An Autumn Afternoon

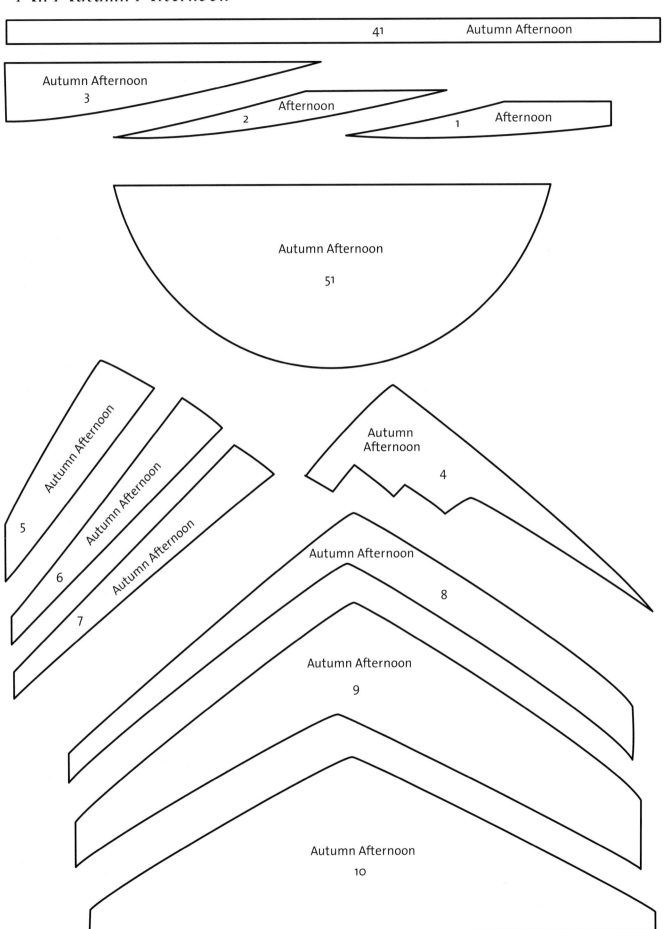

41   Autumn Afternoon

Autumn Afternoon
3

Afternoon
2

Afternoon
1

Autumn Afternoon

51

Autumn Afternoon

5

Autumn Afternoon

6

Autumn Afternoon

7

Autumn
Afternoon

4

Autumn Afternoon

8

Autumn Afternoon

9

Autumn Afternoon

10

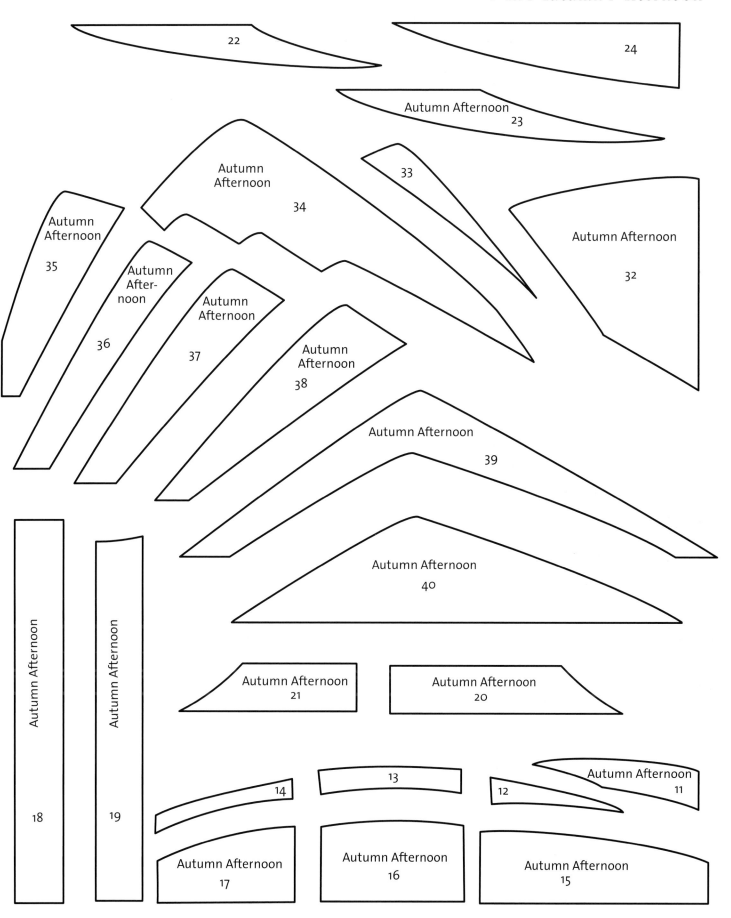

22

24

Autumn Afternoon
23

Autumn
Afternoon
34

33

Autumn Afternoon
32

Autumn
Afternoon
35

Autumn
After-
noon
36

Autumn
Afternoon
37

Autumn
Afternoon
38

Autumn Afternoon
39

Autumn Afternoon
40

Autumn Afternoon

Autumn Afternoon

Autumn Afternoon
21

Autumn Afternoon
20

Autumn Afternoon
18

Autumn Afternoon
19

14

13

Autumn Afternoon
11

12

Autumn Afternoon
17

Autumn Afternoon
16

Autumn Afternoon
15

113

An Autumn Afternoon

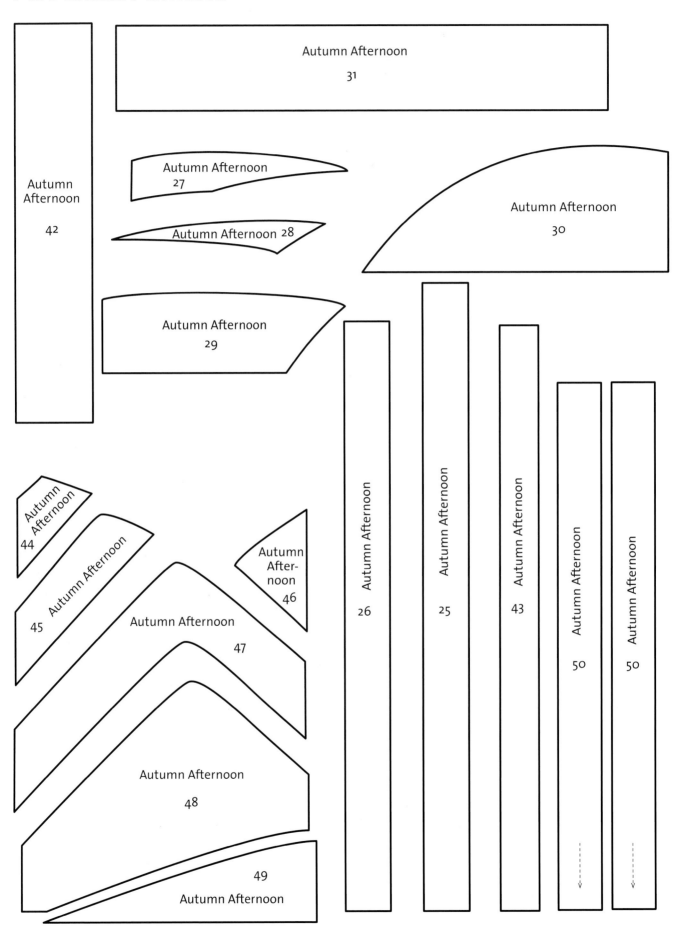

Autumn Afternoon 31

Autumn Afternoon 42

Autumn Afternoon 27

Autumn Afternoon 28

Autumn Afternoon 30

Autumn Afternoon 29

Autumn Afternoon 44

Autumn Afternoon 45

Autumn Afternoon 46

Autumn Afternoon 47

Autumn Afternoon 48

Autumn Afternoon 49

Autumn Afternoon

Autumn Afternoon 26

Autumn Afternoon 25

Autumn Afternoon 43

Autumn Afternoon 50

Autumn Afternoon 50

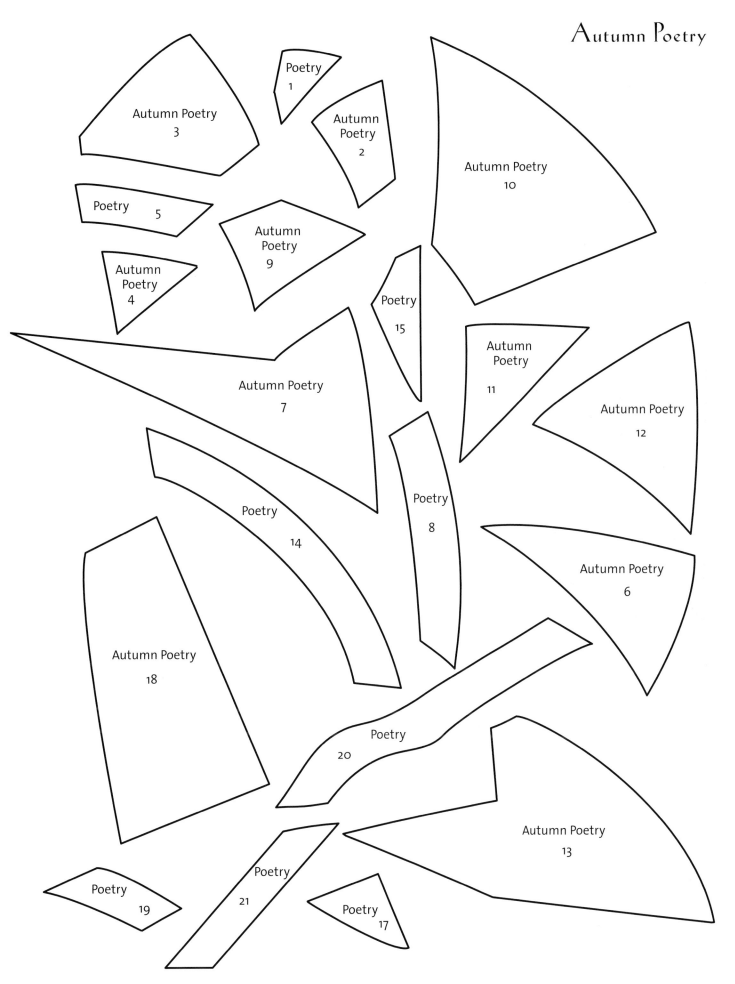

Autumn Poetry

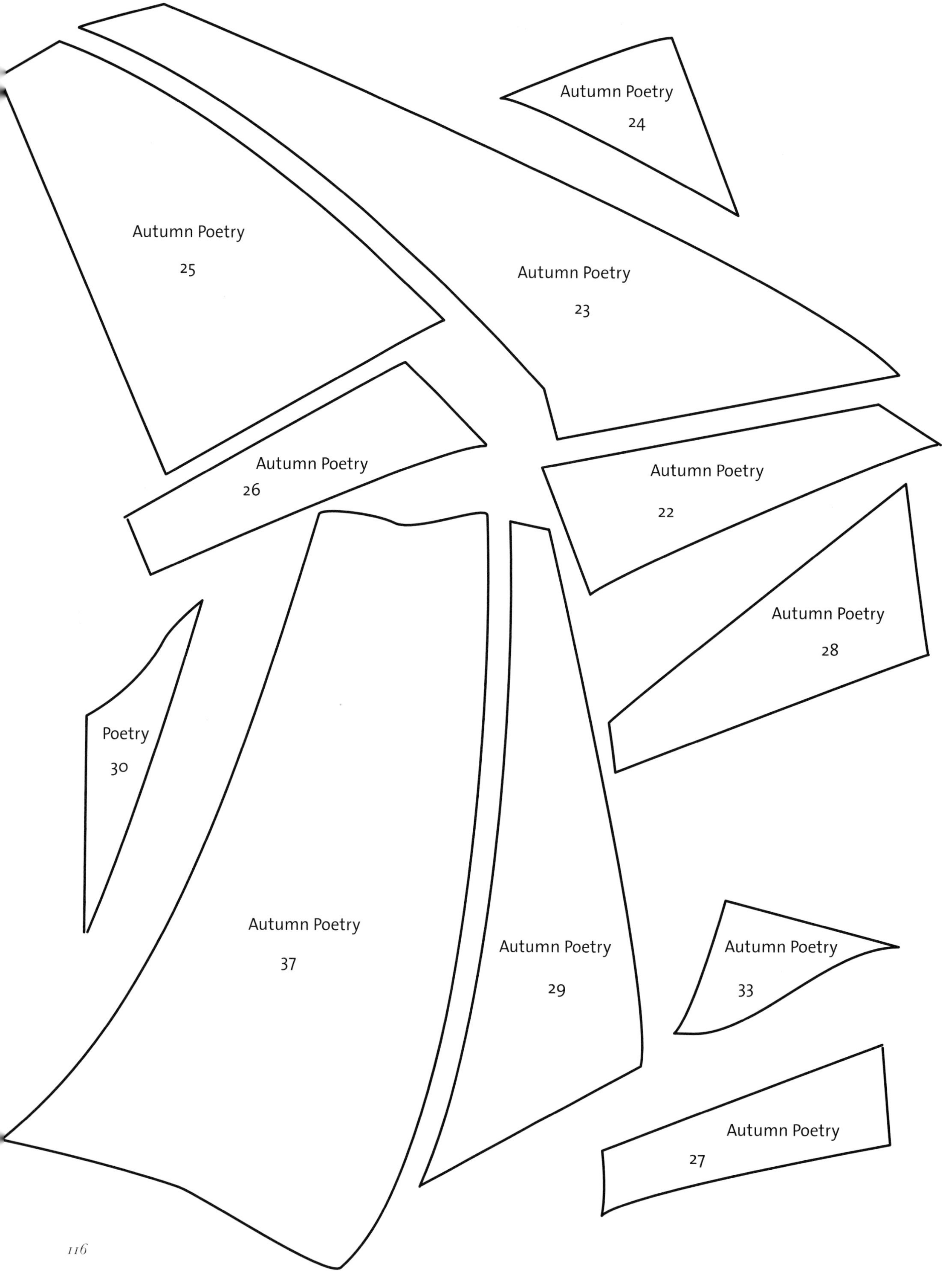

Autumn Poetry

Autumn Poetry

24

Autumn Poetry

25

Autumn Poetry

23

Autumn Poetry

26

Autumn Poetry

22

Autumn Poetry

28

Poetry

30

Autumn Poetry

37

Autumn Poetry

29

Autumn Poetry

33

Autumn Poetry

27

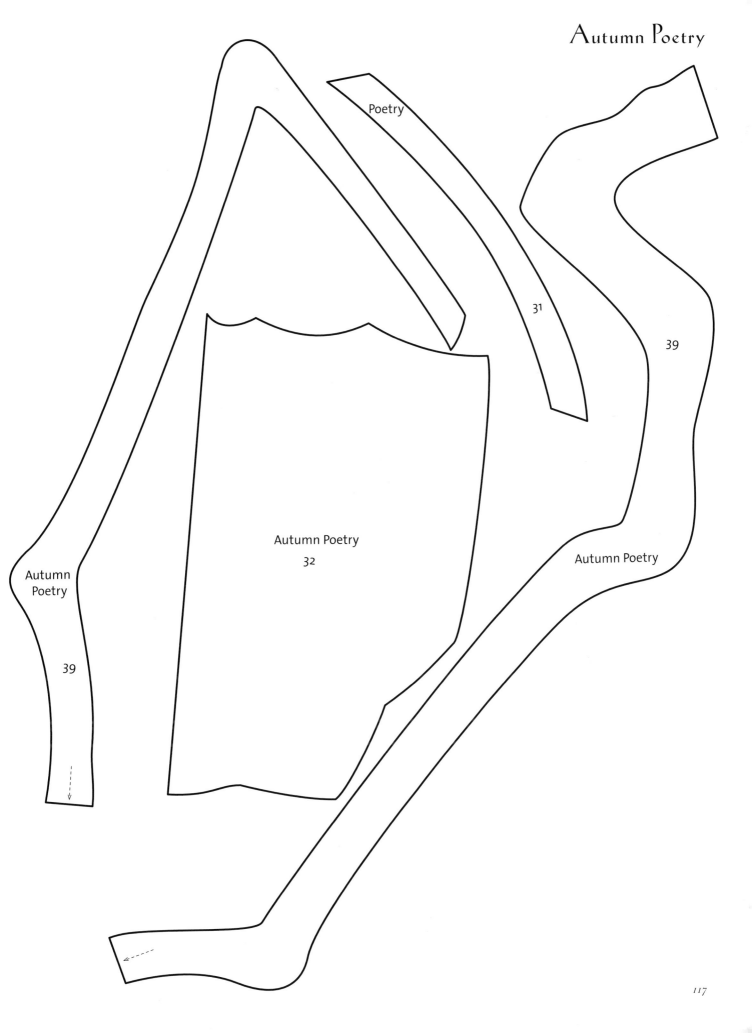

Poetry

31

39

Autumn Poetry
32

Autumn
Poetry
39

Autumn Poetry

Autumn Poetry

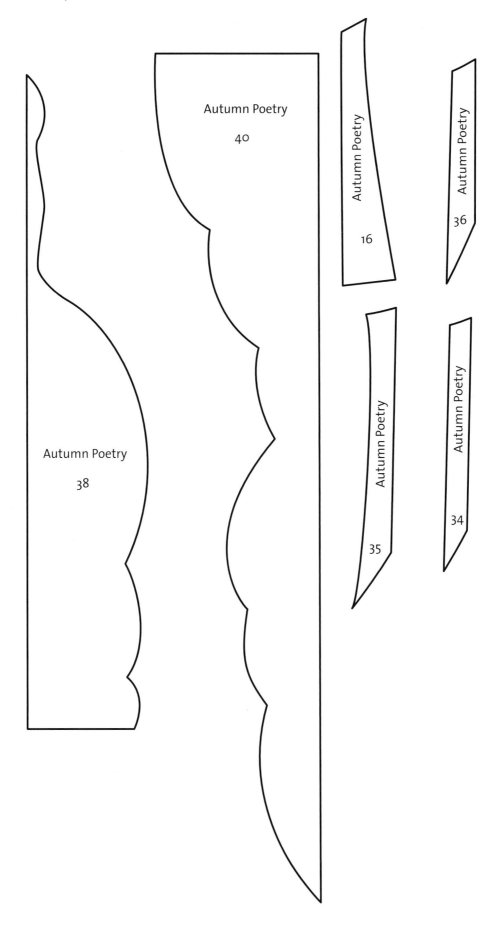

Autumn Poetry

40

Autumn Poetry

38

Autumn Poetry

16

Autumn Poetry

36

Autumn Poetry

35

Autumn Poetry

34

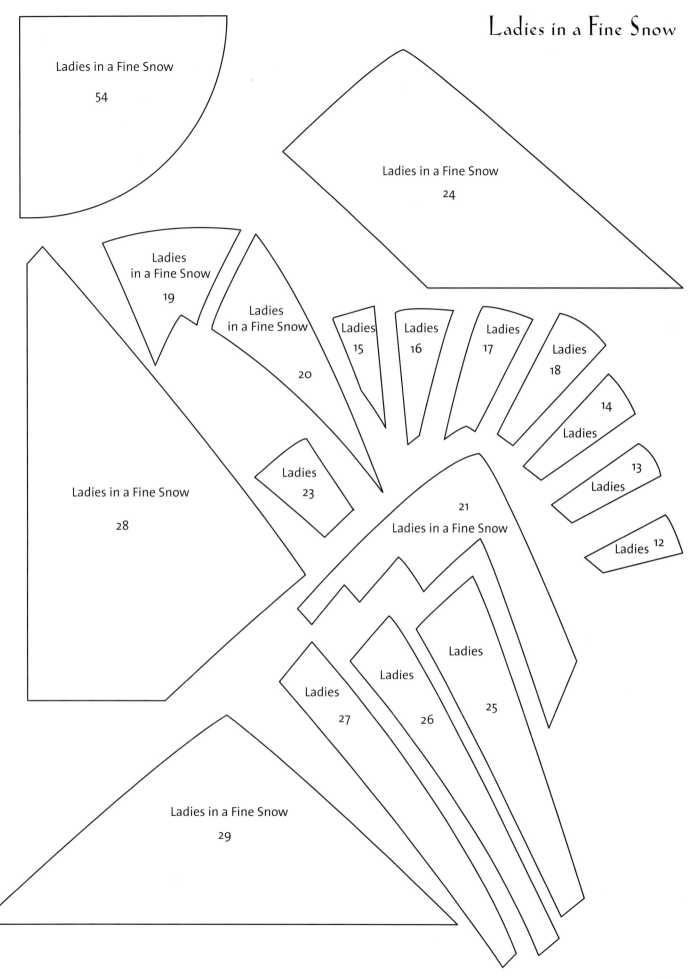

Ladies in a Fine Snow

Ladies in a Fine Snow
54

Ladies in a Fine Snow
24

Ladies
in a Fine Snow
19

Ladies
in a Fine Snow
20

Ladies
15

Ladies
16

Ladies
17

Ladies
18

Ladies
14

Ladies
13

Ladies 12

Ladies
23

Ladies in a Fine Snow
21

Ladies in a Fine Snow
28

Ladies
27

Ladies
26

Ladies
25

Ladies in a Fine Snow
29

Ladies in a Fine Snow

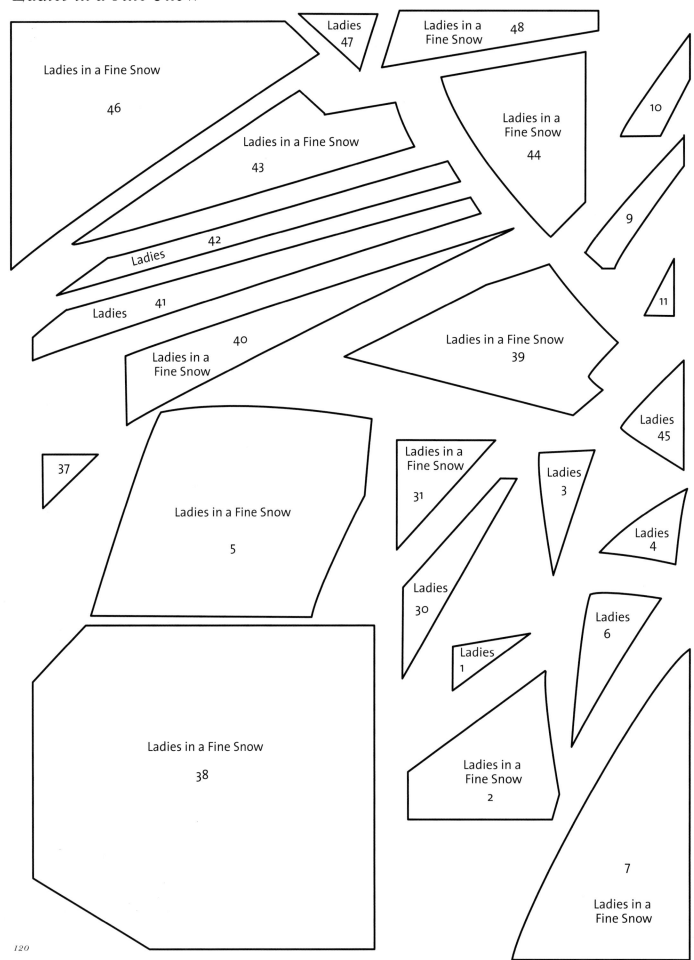

Ladies
47

Ladies in a
Fine Snow   48

Ladies in a Fine Snow

46

Ladies in a Fine Snow

43

Ladies in a
Fine Snow

44

10

9

11

Ladies

42

Ladies

41

Ladies in a Fine Snow

39

Ladies

40

Ladies in a
Fine Snow

Ladies
45

37

Ladies in a Fine Snow

5

Ladies in a
Fine Snow

31

Ladies
3

Ladies
4

Ladies

30

Ladies
6

Ladies
1

Ladies in a Fine Snow

38

Ladies in a
Fine Snow

2

7

Ladies in a
Fine Snow

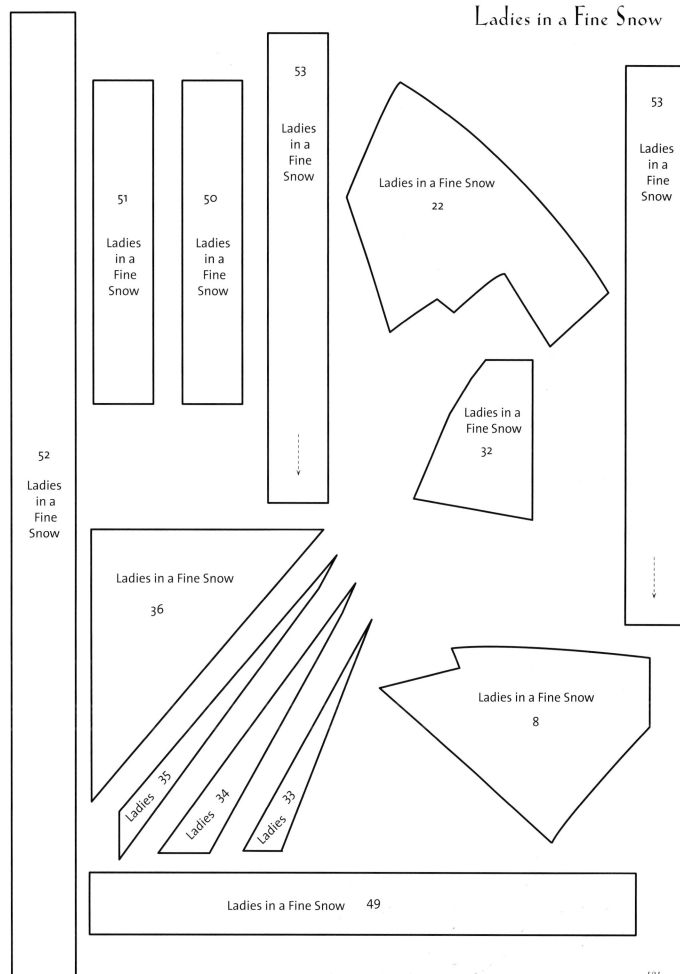

The Silvery Moon over the River

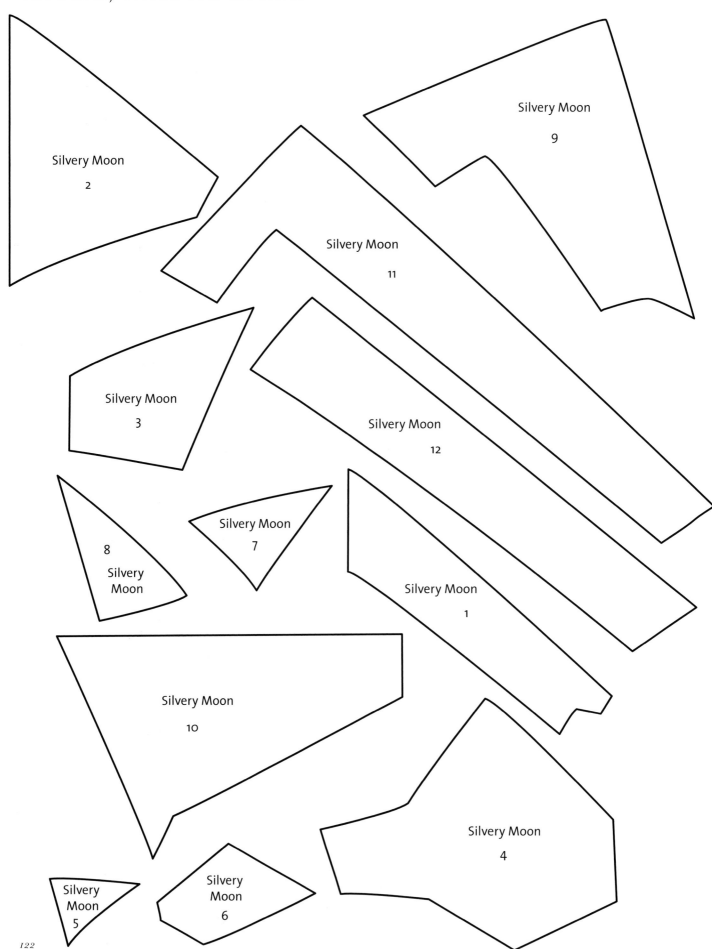

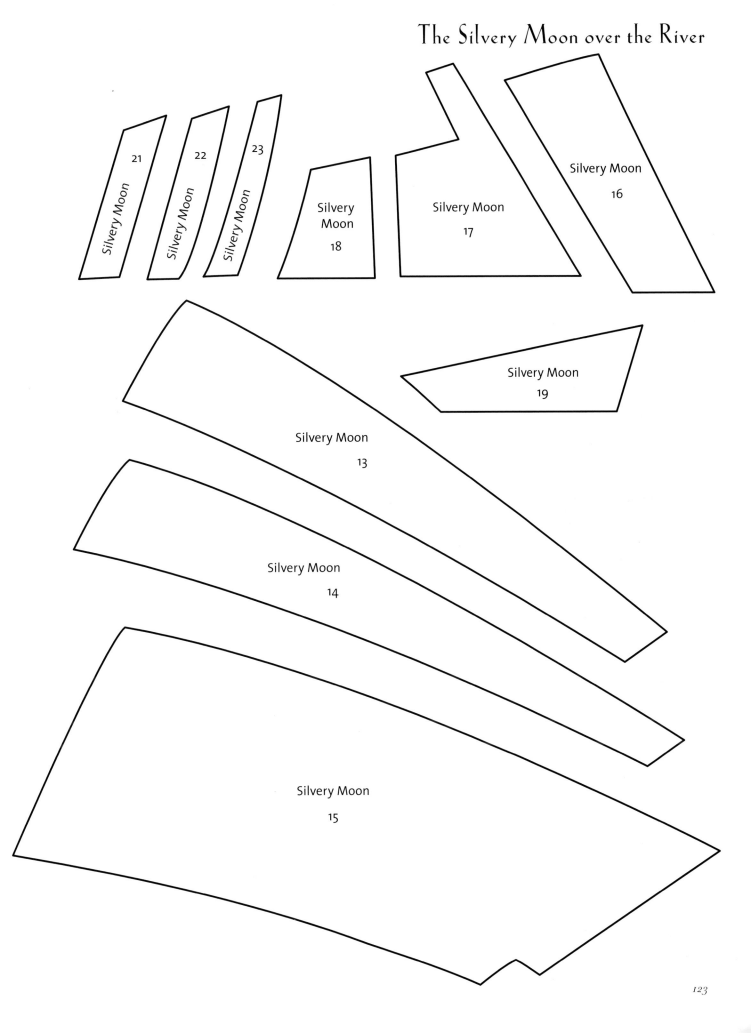

Silvery Moon 21

Silvery Moon 22

Silvery Moon 23

Silvery Moon 18

Silvery Moon 17

Silvery Moon 16

Silvery Moon 13

Silvery Moon 19

Silvery Moon 14

Silvery Moon 15

The Silvery Moon over the River

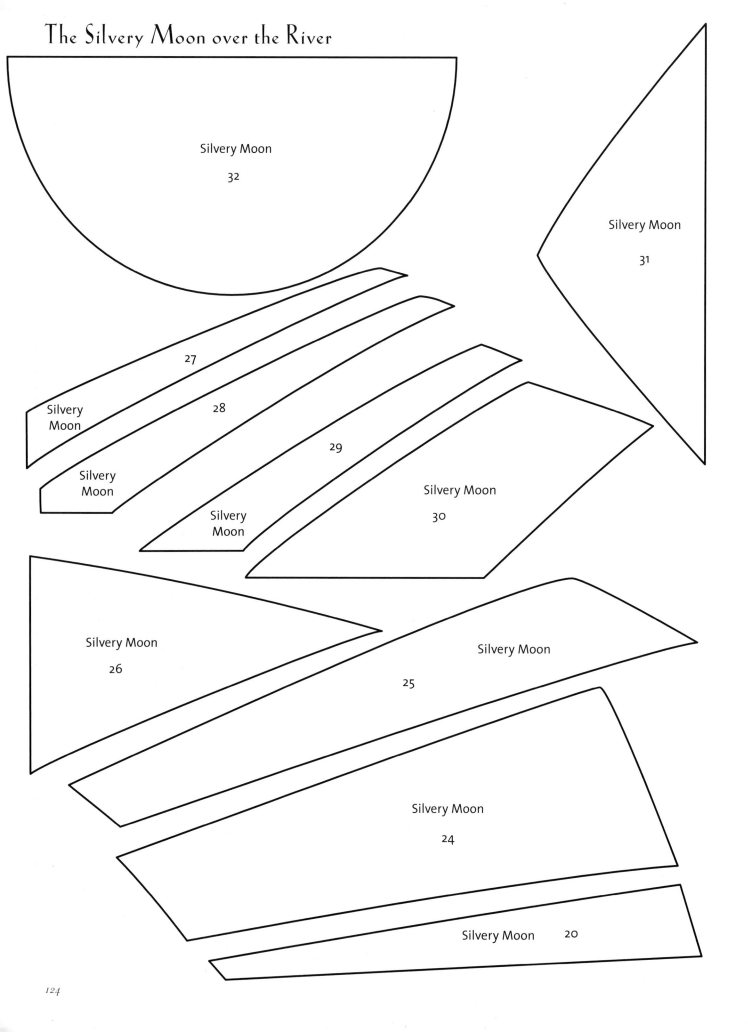

Silvery Moon

32

Silvery Moon

31

27

Silvery
Moon

28

Silvery
Moon

Silvery
Moon

29

Silvery Moon

30

Silvery Moon

26

Silvery Moon

25

Silvery Moon

24

Silvery Moon   20

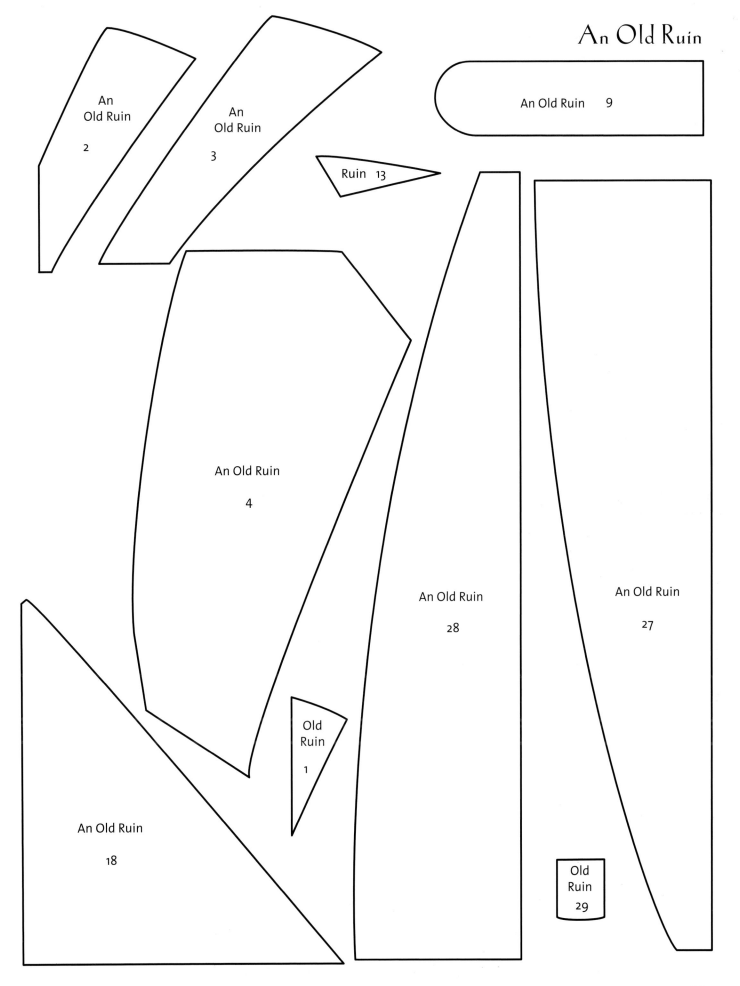

An Old Ruin

An
Old Ruin
2

An
Old Ruin
3

An Old Ruin   9

Ruin   13

An Old Ruin
4

An Old Ruin
28

An Old Ruin
27

Old
Ruin
1

An Old Ruin
18

Old
Ruin
29

An Old Ruin

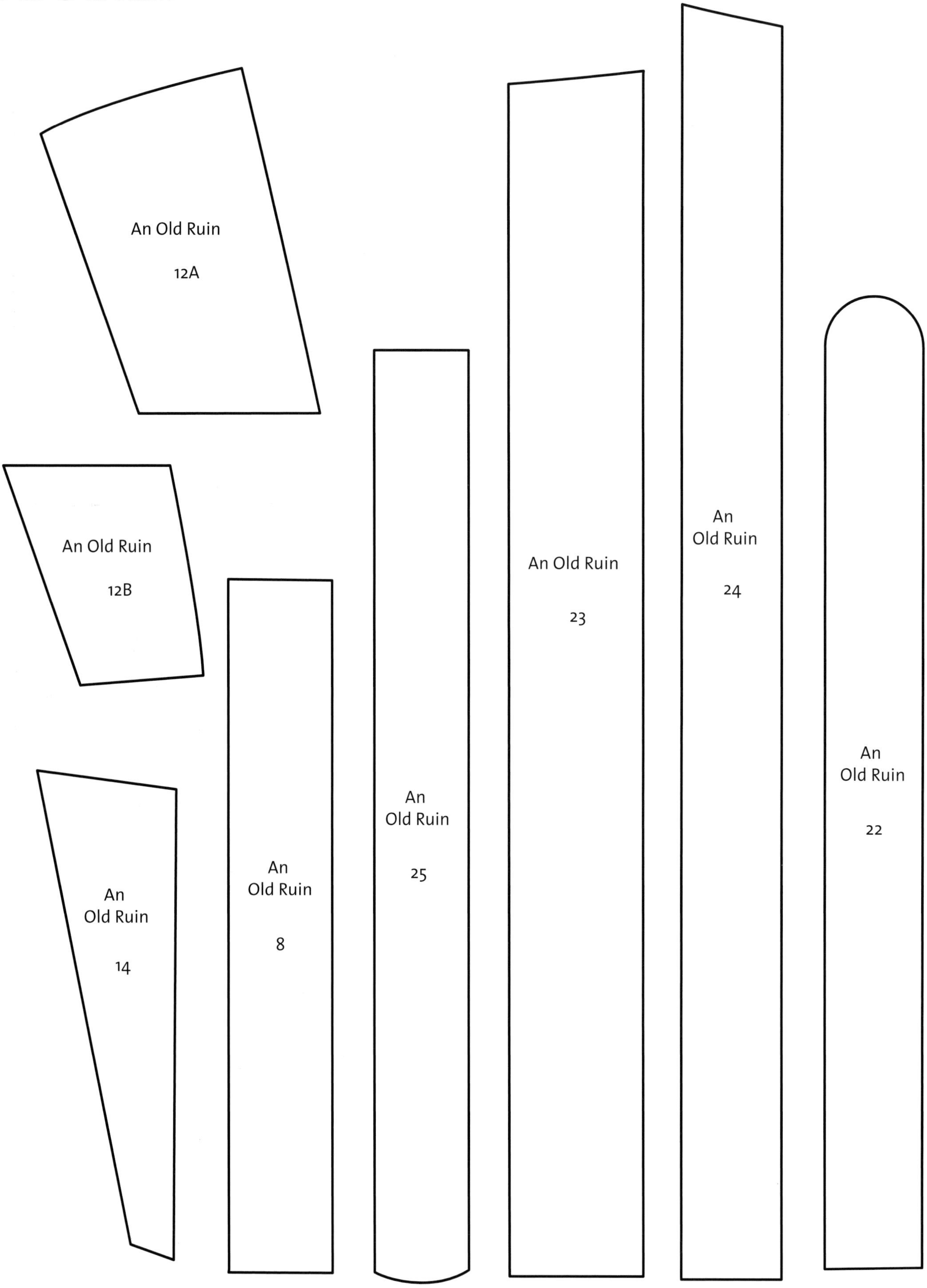

An Old Ruin

12A

An Old Ruin

12B

An
Old Ruin

14

An
Old Ruin

8

An
Old Ruin

25

An Old Ruin

23

An
Old Ruin

24

An
Old Ruin

22

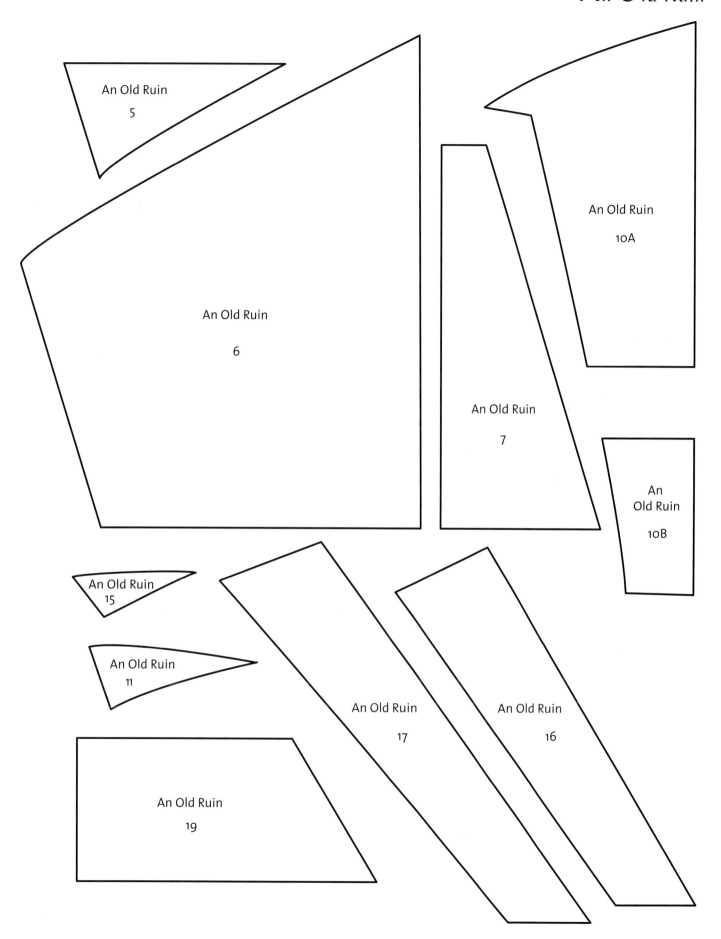

An Old Ruin
5

An Old Ruin
6

An Old Ruin
7

An Old Ruin
10A

An
Old Ruin
10B

An Old Ruin
15

An Old Ruin
11

An Old Ruin
17

An Old Ruin
16

An Old Ruin
19

An Old Ruin

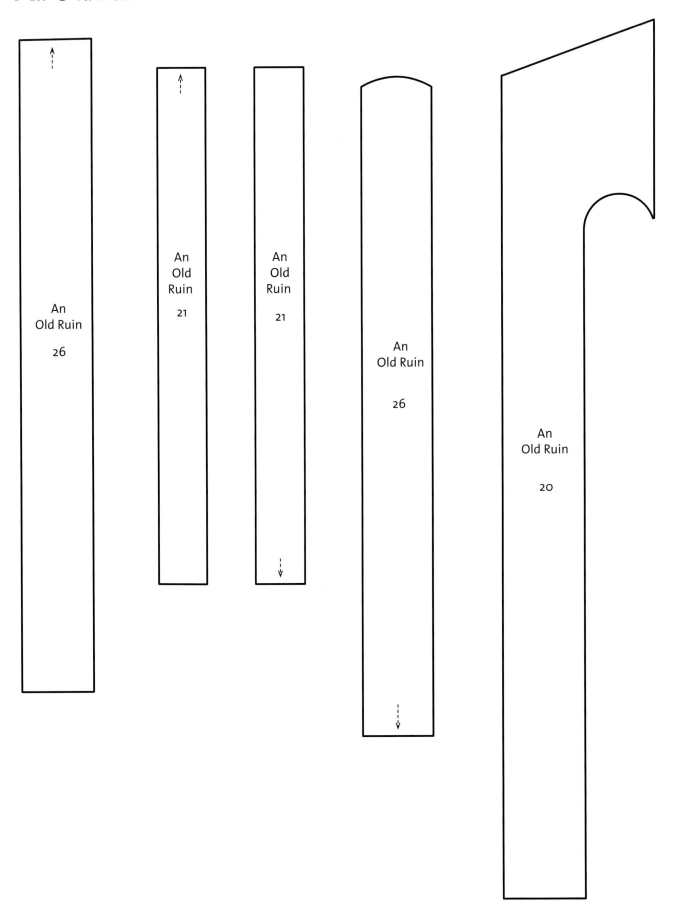

An
Old Ruin

26

An
Old
Ruin

21

An
Old
Ruin

21

An
Old Ruin

26

An
Old Ruin

20

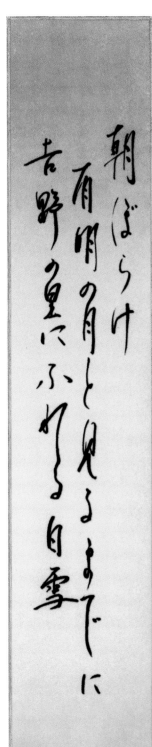

Lesson Plan

When the late autumn wind from Mount Yoshino blows in the deep evening, it heralds a severe, cold night. There are distant sounds in the silence. Perhaps a woman is at work late into the night, preparing for the winter. As I take a break in my journey at a quiet inn, I enjoy a touch of the loneliness of life.

A *waka* poem by Kumiko Sudo.
Inspired by *Ladies in a Fine Snow*,
page 91.

Lesson Plan

Here are suggestions for a one-day workshop, "Making a Miniature Quilt: Moonlit Night." During this sample lesson, students will make one of the simpler miniatures featured in *Harmonies & Hurricanes*. The process includes learning to work with templates, learning and practicing a precise method of hand appliqué, and looking at colors and fabrics in a new way.

First Hour

Give each student one or more photocopies of the diagram for *Moonlit Night* (page 73). Discuss Kumiko's color and fabric use, pointing out colors that add excitement and colors that bring harmony to the overall design. Discuss the concept of balance. Help students begin their own color and fabric selections by reviewing contrast of light and dark colors, texture, movement, and the use of bold fabrics with large designs. Instruct students to color their diagrams, to experiment

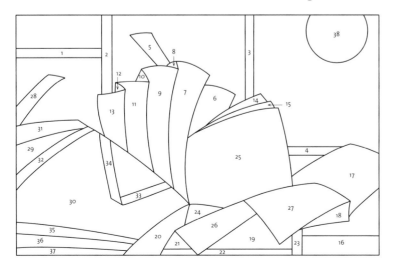

with colors of their choosing, and then to make their final decisions about the colors they will use.

Second Hour

Students trace the template pattern pieces on pages 106 to 108 onto white paper. Have them label and cut out each one. Remind students that the pattern pieces do not include seam allowances. Discuss any changes students may want to make to Kumiko's layout of *Moonlit Night,* and help them make any new templates they need.

Third Hour

After discussing the type of fabric to be used for the project, students select the fabrics that they will need to match their color sketches as closely as possible. Following the steps on page 75, students cut the fabric piece for the background.

Supply List

Appliqué needles

Thread

Straight pins

Paper and fabric scissors

Tracing paper

Ruler

Pencil

Colored pencils

Thimble

Fabric marker

White drawing paper

Notebook

Background fabric

Fabric for quilt top

Border fabric

Batting

Backing fabric

Fourth and Fifth Hours

Students lay the pattern pieces (without seam allowance) on the fabric pieces and draw around the edges with the fabric marker, indicating the seam line. In the sequence shown in the diagrams on pages 75 to 77, students begin to appliqué the fabric pieces to the back-ground. Have them double-check, using the pattern pieces, that each sewn fabric piece is the right size before going on to the next piece.

Sixth Hour

Have students experiment by holding different border fabrics against their quilt tops before making a border fabric decision. Have students make the borders and sew them to the quilt top. Students first join the top, batting, and backing with basting stitches. Discuss the amount of quilting students wish to add to their quilts—along the borders only, following the seam lines, freeform design, etc.—and have students begin quilting accordingly. Add binding, if desired.

Bibliography

The Art Institute of Chicago. *Five Centuries of Japanese Kimono.* Chicago: The Art Institute of Chicago, 1992.

Dalby, Lisa. *Kimono Fashioning Culture.* New Haven and London: Yale University Press, 1993.

De Mente, Boyé Lafayette. *Japan Encyclopedia.* Chicago: Passport Books, 1995.

Reischauer, Edwin O. *The Japanese.* Tokyo: Charles E. Tuttle Co., 1978.

Shikibu, Murasaki. *The Tale of Genji.* Translated by Arthur Waley. Tokyo: Charles E. Tuttle Co., 1970.

Yanagi, Soetsu. *The Unknown Craftsman: A Japanese Insight into Beauty.* Tokyo: Kodansha International, 1972.